MIDDLE KINGDOM ART

in ANCIENT EGYPT

For behold, I have had a statue of myself fashioned upon this boundary which I have made not only that you may prosper on account of it, but also that you may fight for it.

King Senusret III: *Second Semna Stela,* 1865 B.C.

Even the sculptures of the time sought to bring out this emphasis on conscientious character and moved from a delineation of majesty and force to a portrayal of concern for obligations. Such careworn portraits of the pharaohs of the Middle Kingdom are well known.

John A. Wilson: in *Before Philosophy,* 1949.

MIDDLE KINGDOM
ART
IN
ANCIENT EGYPT
2300—1590 B.C.

by
CYRIL ALDRED

1956
ALEC TIRANTI LTD.
72 CHARLOTTE STREET
LONDON, W.1

PUBLISHERS' ACKNOWLEDGMENT

The Publishers wish to express their thanks to the EGYPTIAN EXPLORATION SOCIETY of London for their kind assistance and encouragement, and to their old friend, George W. Allan, of Cairo, for his great help.

They also wish to thank the EGYPTIAN MINISTRY OF FOREIGN AFFAIRS and G. W. Allan for the use of plates 8, 21, 36, 64, 72, 73, 77, 79 and 82.

First published 1950.
Reprinted 1956.

Made and printed in Britain

PREFACE

Die bildende Kunst ist die direkteste Sprache Agyptens—*H. G. Evers.*

The main difficulty that faces the writer of a book of this scope is where to draw the line. The Ancient Egyptian adorned so much of what he touched that very little can be excluded from a survey of his art. In this book, however, as in its companion volume, the main emphasis has been placed upon sculpture, which is the most forceful and characteristic expression of the artistic genius of the Egyptian, and which alone can provide a common standard for measuring the development of his æsthetic ideas throughout the ages. As the writer's concern is as much with these ideas as with their modes of expression, he makes no apology for shading his eyes in order to see further. While, therefore, some will doubtless deplore that architecture, painting and the applied arts should have been excluded, or treated too summarily, the ordinary reader is recommended to consult the works cited in the short bibliography for further guidance. If this little book should throw its modest beam thus far, its purpose will have been sufficiently served.

In the main, it has not been found necessary to depart from the attributions of sculpture worked out by Dr. Evers in his *Staat aus dem Stein*—a notable instance of the methods of *Kunstwissenschaft* applied to Egyptological problems. For the chronology and history of the period, the views advanced by Herbert E. Winlock in his *Rise and Fall of the Middle Kingdom* have been accepted with little modification.

Finally, the writer would like to thank friends and colleagues in different countries for providing information and suitable photographs, and for securing the permission of their institutions to publish this material. Such courtesy is acknowledged more explicitly in the *Descriptive Notes;* but a special tribute is due to Mr. John D. Cooney of the Brooklyn Museum for much helpful encouragement and for so generously allowing the illustration of unpublished specimens in the magnificent collections in his charge.

EDINBURGH, 1950.   C.A.

vi

CONTENTS

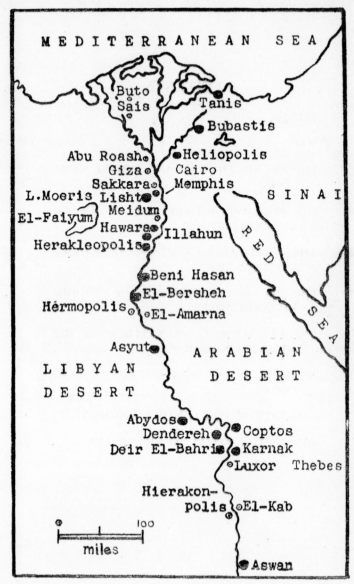

ANCIENT EGYPT, SHOWING THE MAIN SITES.

I.

The Art of the Old and Middle Kingdoms

THE student who examines the arts of the Middle Kingdom of Ancient Egypt with recollections of the Old Kingdom style still vivid in his mind is likely to experience surprise, perhaps bewilderment, as he realises that the artistic climate has undergone a complete change and that a chiller wind is now blowing which freezes rather than animates.

Old Kingdom sculpture, gradually emerging from the regal monumentality of its earlier phase, and expressing movement in a more lively *genre* style as it becomes vulgarised, seems to be wandering towards a limited naturalism when the scene suddenly ends in political collapse. When the curtain rises again in the XIth Dynasty, we are at once aware that an uncompromising formalism has become the plastic ideal. So far from disengaging itself further from its stone matrix, the sculptured form seeks to shrink into it as though for sanctuary. The deceased is no longer shown striding forward, alert, eager, in all the pride of a healthy physique. Instead, lacking such assurance, he has retired into a bleaker contemplation, pulling his cloak around him (Nos. 34, 37, 67, 75). The soft limestone statuary of the Old Kingdom disappears, and there is now a preference for sombre stones which were not coloured for a total effect, but often highly polished for their own sakes (Nos. 41, 44, 69, 81). There is even a contrast in the quantity and size of these hard stone sculptures: while royal statues are large, often colossal, the statuary of private persons tends to be of modest dimensions, even undersized. The athletic musculature that is so characteristic of the semi-nude statuary of the Old Kingdom is now almost prudishly eschewed, and clothing and heavy wigs reduce the human form to a cuboid mass. At the same time, seats and back-pillars, as well as garments and other accoutrements, play an important part in this stylised sculpture, and like the postures that are adopted, seem designed to emphasise the massive, brooding immobility of the statue (Nos. 12, 13, 35, 68, 76). Even carvings in wood, which by their very nature should encourage a more organic style, tend to be formal and a little stiff (Nos. 5, 6, 29). In short, it would hardly be a great exaggeration to claim that during the Middle Kingdom, statuary seems to aspire to the condition of being a pure block of stone (No. 36). It is clear that in almost every aspect the naturalistic ideal of late Old Kingdom art has been rejected in favour of a more abstract formalism.

This is particularly the case with private statuary. The royal statues, while maintaining a more traditional pose, have little of the god-like geniality or even the regality of the Old Kingdom Pharaonic sculptures. The heads that wear the Middle Kingdom crowns lie uneasy; and instead, the expression is almost brutal (Nos. 10, 11, 19), or severe (Nos. 25, 41, 50): at the most sympathetic, it is sad and introspective (Nos. 57, 58, 63, 64). The artist seems to be less concerned with delineating majesty or divinity than with conveying an official mood; less with imprisoning godhead in stone than with releasing human characterisation.

If an explanation of this artistic revolution must be sought, it will be necessary to examine the environment in which Egyptian æsthetic ideas developed during the incubation of the First Intermediate Period, when the culture of the Old Kingdom was replaced by something rather different.

II.

The Religious Background of Middle Kingdom Art

Among the lower layers that we can trace in the ancient rubbish-mound of Egyptian religion is an early belief in a kind of material persistence after death. It is evident that the deceased, or some aspect of him, was thought to pass a ghostly existence in the actual tomb chamber, where he could survive as long as his embalmed corpse was not destroyed, and as long as food-offerings were brought for his subsistence by pious relatives or by the funerary priests who had been endowed for that function. Most of the arts of the Old Kingdom, and indeed of all Pharaonic Egypt—the portrait statues, which could be infused with the spirit of the deceased, the wall paintings or coloured reliefs, perpetuating experiences of the life that was past as incidents of the life to come, even tomb architecture—owe their origin and development to this idea, however modified it may have become with advancing civilisation.

Another form of survival, however, seems to have been permitted to the Pharaoh, who, as a divine king, a god incarnate, alone enjoyed a full and active afterlife among his fellow-deities in the sky-realms. By historic times the royal family and Court had come to partake of this immortality in so far as they had served the king on earth and could be expected to exercise similar offices after death.

The priesthoods of the various local gods attempted from time to time to syncretise many of the different and conflicting beliefs into a theological system in which ideas about the after-life were related to creation myths, and other gods were put into a proper kinship with the supreme local deity. The most successful of these systems was that devised by the priests of the sun-god Ra of Heliopolis; and owing to the zeal, learning and authority of the Heliopolitan college, and the adoption of its eschatology as a royal cult by the Pharaohs of the Vth and VIth Dynasties, the power and prestige of the sun-religion enormously increased, so that even in the Middle Kingdom local gods like Menthu-ra of Armant, Sebek-ra of the Faiyum, and Amen-ra of Thebes found it expedient to become solarised in order to have more than a parochial appeal. But the religion of Ra, like similar sun-cults elsewhere, centred round the king and his entourage, and probably had few adherents outside Court circles, though its forms and rituals set an undying Pharaonic fashion. When the power of the kingship declined towards the end of the old Kingdom, the influence of the sun-cult decayed with it and suffered a severe blow in the anarchy that followed the collapse of the regime.

The history of all human institutions in the Old

Kingdom is the gradual spread to other members of the community of beliefs and privileges that had once been peculiar to the kingship; and this process was greatly accelerated in the First Intermediate Period when the feudal nobility regarded themselves as so many local Pharaohs and took over, with the idea of a kingly after-life in the sky-realms, other royal prerogatives, such as the funerary texts and insignia of authority, as amulets of great power enabling the deceased to open all gates to the other world. By the beginning of the Middle Kingdom the ritual of the sun-cult, which had infused the arts of the Old Kingdom with such life and meaning, had decayed to a mere technique of magic.

There was, however, a rival faith of perhaps equal antiquity which had once come into conflict with the Ra-cult but had later been accepted into the solar pantheon. This was the Osiris-religion. Osiris, who was probably in origin a fertility king who was ceremonially slain by his successor, established himself in pre-dynastic times in the Delta whence his cult spread to other centres, notably to Abydos in Upper Egypt, which eventually became his holy city *par excellence*. The dynastic Osiris was less of a fertility or corn god than the god of the dead—a divine king who had suffered death and resurrection to rule in the other world. The strength of his cult was the promise of immortality which it held out to all men, not merely the elect. Anarchy and revolution, so far from weakening its appeal, tended to strengthen it. The capture of Abydos by the ambitious Theban princes of the early XIth Dynasty, and the promotion of the Osiris-cult as a counter-faith to that of

their Heracleopolitan overlords, increased its prestige; and with the triumph of the Theban monarchy,
Osiris-worship became widespread and continued to
grow in power and esteem throughout the Middle
Kingdom. Its ideas modified funerary beliefs and
practices, though the conservative Egyptian did not
abandon all his outworn tenets, and many ideas
originally peculiar to the sun-cult were assimilated
by the Osiris-faith. But it is clear that during this
period, belief in a material persistence in the tomb
was gradually overlaid by the idea of a spiritual
after-life in the Osirian realms. The portrait statue
ceases, therefore, to be so important as a speaking
likeness of the deceased, and though not entirely dis-
carded, is reduced in size. It is no longer protected
like the vulnerable corpse of its owner in a special
chamber, but is associated with the body itself, being
often placed in the coffin or near it (No. 6). At the
same time the *ex voto,* or temple statue, makes a
more general appearance, particularly at Abydos,
where it enabled the pious to take part in the temple
ceremonies by proxy, and to receive a share of the
offerings (No. 37). It is true that as early as the IVth
Dynasty, in one or two instances, tomb statues were
not hidden away in their serdab-chambers; but such
practices were exceptional during the Old Kingdom,
even in the VIth Dynasty.

It is not perhaps paradoxical that with this dimi-
nution in the importance of the funerary statue, the
corpse of the deceased should now receive a little
more attention, since, like the dismembered body of
Osiris himself, it could be restored to life in the other
world. So there is a tendency, already well-estab-

lished in the Old Kingdom, to trap it out in the mummy bandages of Osiris rather than in the clothes of the living; and to lavish more attention upon its enclosing coffin, making it not in the rectangular shape of the earthly house, but of anthropomorphic form like an image of Osiris himself, wearing even the beard of the god (No. 56). The idealistic portraiture of Old Kingdom statuary is transferred to the coffin mask of the deceased who, as his titles now inform us, has become an Osiris, an Immortal.

Court art, however, was less influenced by the Osiris-cult than by its own traditions. Pyramid tombs continued to be built as royal sepulchres and were surrounded by family mastabas and those of one or two retainers—but on a greatly reduced scale. With the revival of a strong centralised monarchy, and with it the forms of the sun-cult in rather new guises, many of the æsthetic ideas and iconographical features of Old Kingdom royal art also received new life. The king himself as a god was entitled to his own funerary cult; yet the royal statues carved in the form of Osiride pillars (Nos. 11–13), and the rock-hewn cenotaph of Senusret III in the holy city of Abydos, show how strong were the new influences.

There is, however, a great distinction to be made between the spiritual ideas of these rival cults. Sun-worship was a religion of the living, active god of the day-sky, who fought hand to hand with his enemies, to whom darkness was anathema, who was re-born with each dawn, and whose ceremonies were conducted in airy, open courts. The æsthetic ideas generated by such a cult fostered a light, delicate architecture based upon natural forms such as the

7

column imitating a palm tree or a cluster of lotus plants. The statuary produced under the stimulus of sun-worship is similarly naturalistic and of an active life-seeking conception.

The Osiris-faith, on the other hand, was the religion of a resurrected, mummified ancestor-deity, who had passively suffered death at the hands of his foes, and who had to be championed by his wife and son. He had assimilated several death gods in his various cult-centres, and at Abydos ruled over an underworld of cavernous halls and hazardous places.* It would hardly be surprising if the ideas behind such a religion encouraged a more sombre and massive chthonic architecture, and a formalised art style that we have defined elsewhere as " claustrophilic."† Abydene architecture reveals an almost subterranean space-conception, and a strong preference for the square-hewn pier and monolithic masonry. It is perhaps significant that the " block " statue should apparently have its origin at Abydos (see No. 37). This and the Osiride pillar confront us with a statuary in which the deceased is no longer shown with foot advanced, coming boldly forth into the daylight, but on the contrary, resting passive before the judgment-seat in some gloomy hall of the underworld.

III.

The Political Background of Middle Kingdom Art

There is, moreover, a further discrimination to be made between these two religions. The Ra-cult of

---

* According to the Lower Egyptian view, the Osirian realms were conceived of as an ideal region of fertile islands reached by boat.
† See *Old Kingdom Art in Ancient Egypt*, p. 10.

Heliopolis was a Lower Egyptian religion, whereas the Osiris-cult of Abydos was an Upper Egyptian faith.

This distinction is not unimportant. Since earliest times, Egypt has consisted of two lands—Upper Egypt in the south with its narrow strip of cultivation between arid deserts, and lower Egypt in the north with its broader horizons, its more temperate climate and its fertile, diversified landscape. While isolated urban communities developed in Lower Egypt, where the topography encouraged a more individualistic and schismatic outlook, the peoples of Upper Egypt remained racially more homogeneous, economically more inter-dependent, and maintained a greater political cohesion. It was from the south that all the great unifying movements originated, which throughout historic times welded the two lands into a highly organised state after periods of anarchy: and we must assume that such powers of organisation arose from a definite attitude of mind on the part of the southerner.

If the north differed from the south in its environmental, economic and ethnic aspects, it would not be over-rash to assume for it on circumstantial grounds alone, a differing artistic vision. Most observers have detected a dualism in Egyptian art to match the dualism in Egyptian culture—an hieratic formalism on the one hand and a more lyrical naturalism on the other. Some have sought to explain this antithesis by suggesting that a popular or folk art existed by the side of a court art, a viewpoint which disregards the conditions of patronage under which the hereditary artist-craftsman worked, and his position

9

in his social *milieu*. It seems more valid from the viewpoint of the art-historian to ascribe this dichotomy to the differences between a northern and a southern cultural pattern. This fundamental duality manifests itself in many ways: the two lands were never really integrated politically, but merely juxtaposed. Only the office of kingship kept them joined together: their institutions remained separate, and whenever the central authority weakened, the two parts flew asunder.

The less artificial life of the north, lived more in sympathy with a gentler, pastoral environment, may have encouraged a more naturalistic art as compared with the more formal style of the disciplined, warlike and harsher south. Unfortunately it is easier to postulate the existence of a northern cultural style than to define all its features. The alluvia of Lower Egypt have not yielded antiquities in such profusion as the dry sands of Upper Egypt; and we cannot as yet isolate a specifically northern dynastic art style. Moreover, the very nature of the union between north and south under the crown made imperative an amalgam, if not a synthesis of any differing cultural styles, just as it was equally politic to conjoin the regalia and the royal titularies. The strength of the Pharaoh's position must have been that he was above regional loyalties. As art in Egypt owed its development to royal patronage, and was entirely dependent upon it in the early Old Kingdom at least, Pharaonic art set the fashion and the pace; and gained enormous authority from being the archetype to which other dynasties returned, no matter what their cultural origin may have been, when once more, after periods of separation, the two kingdoms were united again and all the traditions of regality re-established. Evidence for this is not lacking in the Middle Kingdom—Old Kingdom reliefs were copied both by kings and commoners; Senusret I seems to have revived a Mykerinus type of Hathor triad, if we are to judge from a fragment found at Karnak; Amen-em-het II re-introduced the Kheops or Khephren form of a " three-stripe " wig-cover (cp. No. 40); and Nefer-hetep I searched the archives for a proper representation of the statue of Osiris when he wished to honour that god in Abydos. Antiquarianism, in fact, is a feature of Egyptian art at all periods.

In this way a traditional iconography, fixed in the early Old Kingdom, was inspired and sustained by the patronage of the kings who naturally employed the best craftsmen on their ambitious undertakings. The work of these master-craftsmen was copied for humbler patrons by less skilful men whose accomplishment was measured in so far as they came near the fashion set by royalty. Hence a mean was established, which is perhaps the most characteristic feature of Egyptian Pharaonic art. But even in the work of the royal craftsmen it is possible to detect an interpretation of the norm according to the bias of a particular culture, whether it be of the north or south. It is not difficult, for instance, to recognise the duality of Middle Kingdom court art in the existence of two main schools of sculpture, which may be most conveniently defined as a northern Memphite and a southern Theban school. It is true that the Middle Kingdom also saw the emergence of a number of

11

provincial art centres, which, starting under the inspiration of a court style, developed under the patronage of local lords upon more or less independent lines: but our concern is not primarily with these dwindling off-shoots from the main tradition.

We must also be careful not to confuse such stylistic identifications with geographical provenance. An antiquity from a northern site, will not necessarily have been made in Lower Egypt, especially if it be of royal workmanship. It is necessary to emphasise this truism, for instance, because the finding of a number of royal statues at Tanis in the Delta has been held sufficient reason for identifying a Tanite school of sculpture quite distinct in its features from any other school, even of northern origin (cp. No. 77). But in the case of royal sculpture we must assume that the craftsmen lived wherever the Court was located, and were despatched under the supervision of a high official to any particular site. The style and details of the reliefs of Menthu-hetep III at Tod, Elephantine, and Armant, for instance, are so similar that it is almost certain that they were executed by the same group of artists.

In the XIth Dynasty the capital was in Upper Egypt at Thebes, which maintained an importance during most of the period; and XIth Dynasty art is virtually an Upper Egyptian style, powerful and somewhat abstract in its emphasis upon underlying cubic forms. In the XIIth Dynasty, although the administrative centre was shifted to the Faiyum, and although we may assume that it was here that the best artists from north and south were employed in the royal workshops, the dynasty long preserved its

Theban connections. Its kings may have had more than a dash of Nubian blood in their veins: at least they were anxious to claim princes of Thebes as their ancestors. Middle Kingdom art, in fact, is largely of southern inspiration. The naturalism of the Memphite style may leaven here and there the more massive works of the Theban school, and may inform the more idealistic funerary sculpture, but no longer does it predominate: and we must ascribe the restrained, volumetric conception of form in the Middle Kingdom to an aggressive Upper Egyptian element in the culture of the period.

The Egyptian, as a result of foreign infiltration in the First Intermediate Period, had become more conscious of his national culture: and there is some evidence in the Court art of the Middle Kingdom for the expression of a new idea—the concept of the Egyptian State with the Pharaoh as its administrative chief as well as its spiritual head. It is less the divinity of the ruler that we are now aware of than his regality. What saved the Pharaoh from becoming another impotent Mikado was the territorial ambitions of the Theban princes of the early XIth Dynasty who linked their interests with the political supremacy of the State. War becomes an instrument of State policy and is no longer left to the local vassal to wage on his lord's account: the expeditions that were now sent abroad more often than not had the Pharaoh at their head as commander-in-chief. The ideas of statecraft that monarchs left for the instruction of their sons at this period show a keener appreciation of the duties of the ruler to his people than of the obligations of the people to their god-king. The building of a colossal stone pyramid, requiring all the resources of the State, for the indirect benefit of the people through the welfare of their divine Pharaoh, is no longer possible in the changed times of the Middle Kingdom, though it is true that the funerary temple of Amen-em-het III was enormous. Instead, it is the considerable engineering works of the Faiyum that are undertaken for the direct prosperity of the land and the people.

This political re-orientation had a subtle effect upon the arts of the time. With the integration of the country under a central administration, and with more widespread temple building not only in Egypt itself but also outside its borders, the statue of the king in the local shrine became a reminder as much of the supreme central power as of the divinity of the monarch—the intermediary between the god and its worshippers is also the personification of secular law and order. Royal statuary, in fact, expands its magico-religious significance to include the idea of the personality of the Man and the power of the State. Thus Senusret III erected a statue of himself as a symbol of Egyptian national might upon such dangerous ground as a disputed frontier in Nubia— a changed policy, indeed, from the ancient practice of protecting the sculpture in the sealed serdab-chamber or behind the doors of the temple shrine.

May we not therefore say that by the time of the XIIth Dynasty, royal statuary has overlaid its magico-religious content with other meanings which render it little different in intention from the sculpture of modern times? While we must distinguish statuary which is primarily religious in its form and

14

purpose in the Old Kingdom style, we must also identify sculpture which, though fashioned after the same traditions, is concerned with impressing the beholder with the awe and majesty of the ruler as head of the Egyptian State (cp. Nos. 28, 46).

IV.

The Social Background of Middle Kingdom Art

It was not only outside the borders of Egypt that the central authority had to impose its awesome power. The upheavals of the First Intermediate Period, with its foreign invasion, anarchy and destitution, had left a profound mark upon the structure of Egyptian society and its opinions. The new world was no longer so brave. The pyramids and tombs of sacred kings and their mighty lords had been robbed and desecrated despite all the proverbial wisdom of such famous men. A mood of disillusion and deep resignation suffuses the thought of the period. The contemporary literature is pessimistic, even cynical; and the precepts that certain kings left for the guidance of their posterity reveal a shrewd appreciation of the shortcomings of human nature, and while counselling justice and propriety, advise also scepticism and vigilance. Joy in a successful earthly life, which had inspired the arts of the Old Kingdom with such fresh and exuberant vitality, was replaced by a more sober belief in an ideal equalitarian existence, which could be achieved only in the after-life as a result of good works and pious living. This restraint is reflected in the quiescent art of the Middle Kingdom, and gazes out from the sad faces

15

with their heavy-lidded eyes that we see in the portrait statues.

The most striking effect of the social revolution was a changed attitude to the monarchy which had suffered a loss of prestige. The Pharaoh was still sacrosanct, of course, and as such, very dangerous with the high destructive potential that his divinity induced in him; but he was no longer unique, since his god-like state could be attained by all his subjects in the Osirian hereafter. The local governors had usurped many of the royal prerogatives, and although the Theban princes eventually gained control of a united land, it was evident that the kingship could easily change hands: either Menthu-hetep IV or Amen-em-het I was a usurper, if both were not, and the latter seems to have been murdered in a palace intrigue. It was necessary for such dynasts to reward their supporters with local governorships; and a factious, restless feudal class was re-created, which later Senusret III, relying upon popular support, seems to have found it necessary to dispossess. Not till the latter part of the period, in fact, does the prestige of the Pharaoh appear to reach its former limits; and then, while Senusret III, like Senusret I before him, is praised as the superman who keeps the land free from violence, his son, Amen-em-het III is hailed as a god who illumines the earth more than the sun.

This superhumanity is expressed in the realistic portrait sculpture of the age. Colossal sculptures emphasise the might of the central power and the Pharaoh's towering stature above his feudal lords. However traditional the pose may be, the dour features are now not so much those of the inheritor of divine office as those of the vigorous terrestrial ruler, holding the throne against all comers and justifying his possession of it by his actions. The ruthless countenances of these kings are cast in the same mould that autocrats have usually chosen to overawe their less reliable followers. Towards the end of the XIIth Dynasty, however, as the throne won a greater security and a greater loneliness by suppressing or curbing the power of the local lords, the expression of severity becomes softened into melancholy and introspection, even into weariness.

Another result of the ferment caused by social change was the emergence of a middle class of skilled craftsmen, minor scribes and government officials. It was the little man who steadily improved his position throughout the period. The artist, as a member of this class, is no longer quite so anonymous, and several names from this period have survived. The appearance of this new class of patron, however, tended to lower the standards of taste. Quantity was only supplied at a sacrifice of quality, and a cheap kind of derivative art appears which is produced by inferior craftsmen for the *ex votos* and stelae that all pious men who could afford to do so erected at Abydos and elsewhere. Such craftsmen usually copied the simpler, stylised statues on a smaller scale, showing the deceased squatting in a garment which reduces his body to a cuboidal form. Shopwork of this kind, which required very little skilled carving except in the features of the head, varies in quality from the mediocre to the frankly crude. It can give an entirely wrong impression of the standards of the time, unless it be remembered that most of it was produced for a client who formerly had not existed, or had been supplied only by the bounty of his lord.

V.

*The Development of Art during the Middle Kingdom**

The monuments of the Middle Kingdom have suffered cruelly from the fury of conquerors and the cupidity or indifference of later rulers so that a complete survey of the art of the period is hardly possible. Of the architecture, all that now exists is a small but charming processional kiosk of Senusret I, recently reconstructed at Karnak; and a modest shrine of Amen-em-het III and IV, lately uncovered at Medinet Madi in the Faiyum. The temple of Menthu-hetep II at Deir el-Bahri is a mere heap of ruins, and only a few stones now remain of the vast funerary temple of Amen-em-het III at Hawara, which was probably the largest building that the world has yet seen. Relief sculpture after the reign of Senusret I is exceedingly scanty and hardly representative. In the series of royal statues there are important gaps which it does not seem possible to fill; and too many of the masterpieces which have survived are grievously mutilated.

Despite this, however, it is clear that Middle Kingdom art had its beginnings in the local styles that arose in the south as provincial echoes of the Court

* This section should be read in conjunction with the *Descriptive Notes* on pages 33 to 56.

art of Memphis. After the fall of the Old Kingdom (c. 2290 B.C.) these local schools became more isolated and developed along their own lines. Rustic and maladroit as they often were, they sometimes make up for poor sense of proportion and lack of taste by a certain vigour of conception (No. 1). Antiquities from Asyut, which was particularly important as an influential provincial centre, display quite clearly the main features of this art, the suave accomplished Memphite style being re-interpreted in a stiff formalised manner (No. 5). But the statuette of Mesehti, showing the contemporary stone carving, owes little to Old Kingdom models, and in the brutal vigour of its expression, and the abstract, almost " primitive," conception of form, it well reveals the fundamentals that were to underlay the southern inspired art of the Middle Kingdom (No. 3).

The First Intermediate Period was a time of internal warfare, uneasy truces and disunity. Belief in the efficacy of magic increased as the sun-cult decayed; and this and a more widespread poverty encouraged the use of less expensive substitutes for the elaborate tomb equipment of a former age. These new art-forms remained in favour throughout the Middle Kingdom, even with a return of prosperity.

Thus the lively Old Kingdom servant-statues in stone and wood, designed to work for the deceased in some after-life, were now replaced by cheaper wooden figurines and groups which vary in workmanship, the better specimens making good their claim to be considered as works of art (Nos. 7, 38), but the vast majority displaying a crudeness which time has not improved. These figures also seem to

19

have taken over part of the functions of the painted relief (Nos. 30, 55). Their use is only discontinued towards the end of the XIIth Dynasty, perhaps as a result of the complete triumph of the Osiris-faith, which was less materialistic in its concepts and which regarded ploughing, sowing and reaping as exalted privileges rather than menial labours in the after-life.* Another cheap substitute for an object was secured by providing a painted representation of it on the large wooden coffins that now ousted the expensive stone sarcophagi from all but the most sumptuous burials (No. 49). Most of these decorated coffins show an inherent taste and great skill in the disposition and rendering of still-life: they give rise to a tradition which persisted throughout the period and far beyond it. Wall-painting, too, which, with one or two exceptions, had been a second-best substitute for painted relief, now develops as an independent art; and the ruined paintings in the tombs of the viziers Dagi and Antef-oker at Thebes show that it received the highest patronage. The better preserved wall-paintings at Beni Hasan give an indication of how this art-form had developed later in the period, though they are in a local style which is very uneven, and lively rather than accomplished (No. 60).

Art in the Theban area during the XIth Dynasty (2134–1991 B.C.) is best seen in relief sculpture which evolved rapidly from the somewhat timid, though

* The *shabti* figurine which rises in favour as the servant figure declines probably had quite a different function. Anyhow, its duties were confined to clearing irrigation-channels, and spreading the fertile top-soil.

delicate cutting of the early reigns (No. 2) to a high pitch of technical excellence in the sarcophagi of the queens of Menthu-hetep II (Nos. 8, 9). In contemporary statuary there is an obvious difference of standards, though the fact should not be overlooked that few specimens have survived from this period. The statues of Meri are but a feeble reflection of the Memphite style and yet lack the vigour of the Mesehti statuette (No. 4). The wooden figurine of Queen Ashayet is in the tradition of the humble servant statues; but it is from this style of woodcarving that the impressive work of the following generation, and indeed of the XIIth Dynasty, appears to develop (Nos. 6, 7, 29).

With the later statues of Menthu-hetep II we are suddenly faced with an ebullience of this southern school at its most vigorous and intransigent (Nos. 10, 11). The total impression is indeed monumental, not with the regal grandeur of the old style but with a brutal power imposed by force in conformity with the spirit of the age. At Thebes at this time there must have been very little statuary that could have inspired and guided the craftsmen who were thrown back on their own resources, as these statues show. Later relief sculpture of the reign shows much more sophistication, probably because a constant tradition of drawing had been preserved by the ordinary scribal calligraphy. Hieroglyphic-signs are often but the subjects of the relief-scenes greatly reduced; and such scenes in the temples of a former age were easy to copy and reproduce in a way denied to untransportable statues. The few fragments of relief that have been recovered from the ruins of the temple of Menthu-hetep II at Deir el-Bahri, like that monument itself, show a refreshing originality of conception and vigour of execution. The scenes include new and significant subjects showing warfare: and even old subjects are re-interpreted afresh (No. 14). But such shallow relief is little better than drawing. Its hard, precise lines and careful detail produce a raised contour for defining flat areas of colour. In its technique and conception it expresses the same feeling as the carefully defined planes of the cubic sculptures (No. 15).

When Menthu-hetep III ascended the throne, however (2010 B.C.), Egypt had been re-united for a generation. Other traditions and influences were free to diffuse themselves and all the inspiration of the Sakkara reliefs, for instance, could reach the southern capital. What this intercourse may have effected in the field of sculpture cannot, unfortunately, be estimated, since no complete statues have survived; but in relief the fine detail and tight handling of the Theban style seems to have been softened by subtle modelling in the tradition of the royal reliefs of the VIth Dynasty at Sakkara. This is best seen in the sculptures with which Menthu-hetep III decorated temples in his southern domains and which are well represented at Brooklyn by the superb relief from Armant (Nos. 16–18). This standard was hardly surpassed in subsequent reigns, though fragments from Lisht, produced under the inspiration of Old Kingdom models, suggest an equal excellence with rather greater depth. The only development, in fact, that relief sculpture underwent during the remainder of the Middle Kingdom was a much

22

deeper cutting in the reign of Senusret I, when sculptured contours and heavier shadows suggest a return
to the earlier style of Menthu-hetep II at Dendereh,
if indeed its antecedents are not to be sought further
back in the VIth Dynasty (No. 21).

Not until the later reigns were innovations introduced into the Court art of the XIIth Dynasty (Nos.
76, 77). In conformity with the codifying and or-
ganisational character of that age, there was in fact
less original diversity than is apparent in the preceding dynasty; but on the contrary, a tendency to
perfect one or two selected forms. Royal statuary, at
least in its " official " examples, appears to be largely
of Theban inspiration, maintaining the formalistic
vigour and portraiture of the XIth Dynasty style.
The first of a most impressive series of royal portraits,
and in some respects the most striking, is the red
granite colossus of Amen-em-het I (1991–1961 B.C.)
from Tanis, which is one of the only two complete
statues of this king to have been identified (No. 19).

While in the mass the Egyptian appears to have
had rather a different conception of the identity and
personality of a man from what we hold today, there
is little doubt that in the work of the best Court
artists there was a sustained effort to achieve a
portrait in our sense of the term. In the Old Kingdom, portrait statuary had been cast in an idealistic
mould owing to the special part that it played in
the funerary cult; but in the Middle Kingdom, for
the reasons we have already suggested, there was a
tendency to fashion it after a more realistic intention
—to make it larger than life, rather than super-
natural. But in Egypt old ideas died hard; and in

the north the Memphite school seems to have clung to its idealistic traditions with some success throughout the period; the parvenu Theban sculptors, on the other hand, seem to have been more receptive to new influences, and expressed more cogently the spirit of the age, which was so largely of southern inspiration. If careful portraiture was indeed the sculptor's aim, it should be possible to name every royal statue without cavil by its physiognomy. In practice, however, such identifications cannot always be made because strong physical characteristics were transmitted from father to son or grandson. It may also have happened on certain rare occasions that when a king died unexpectedly, a number of his statues and reliefs which were at that moment being finished were inscribed with the name of his successor. Again, the Middle Kingdom custom of associating the heir to the throne as a co-regent may have introduced a sort of unintentional composite portrait, if not a confusion of identities: the Egyptian specialised method of working from one or two master-sculptors' models would make such confusions by no means impossible. The close resemblance of the portraits of Senusret I at Coptos, for instance, to those of his father from the same site seems to require a weightier explanation than that of mere family likeness (No. 22).

With the reign of Senusret I (1961–1927 B.C.), in which the art and culture of the period reached an apogee, there is a pronounced drift from the Theban capital in favour of a centre nearer to the point of political balance at Lisht. But while the Memphite school now seems to have re-established its prestige, there was not at first a synthesis of the two styles, but rather a juxtaposition—the normal Egyptian solution. For while the king undertook extensive funerary construction at Lisht in the north, he also seems to have built or completed a large temple at Karnak to his father's eponymous god, Amen. The portraits of the king from these two sites reveal rather different physiognomies, a broad face with thick lips and wide cheek-bones, as in the Karnak sculptures and reliefs (Nos. 21, 27); and longer, more refined features as in the statues and reliefs from Lisht (Nos. 25, 26). It does not seem possible to account for these distinctions otherwise than by postulating the existence of two separate schools of sculpture, one working in the idealistic funerary tradition of the Old Kingdom, the other in a more realistic official style. To this latter school also seem to belong the hard stone sculptures from Tanis, originally perhaps from Heliopolis or other Delta sites.

The vigorous spirit of this southern school dominates what little sculpture we can identify as belonging to the next two kings. About this time, the stone " block " statue makes its appearance as an *ex voto* (Nos. 36, 37, 75). It does not seem to have had any funerary significance, though it was in one case at least adapted as a tomb statue. It is also unique in not owing its inspiration to a royal arche-type, unless it is the private version of the royal Osiride statue. Block statues quickly grew in favour as temple statues since their simplified forms lent them to mass production as votive offerings for sale to the devout pilgrims at Abydos and other holy

25

c

cities. The cubic nature of this statuary is emphasised as the dynasty advances.

Similar southern inspiration is to be seen in the statues of Senusret II, in which there is an evident attempt to revive the iconography of IVth Dynasty royal sculpture, which itself appears originally to have been of Upper Egyptian, perhaps Abydene inspiration (Nos. 41–47). The spirit of restrained force expressed in this classical sculpture is seen also in the jewellery of the period, much of which has happily survived and affords a survey of the jeweller's craft over several generations. The superb skill and taste of the Egyptian goldsmith at this time have never been surpassed; but a stylistic analysis shows that while in the middle of the dynasty a classical purity of design and perfect technique are the main features of this art, under Senusret III, and still more during the reign of his son, the design begins to lose its simplicity and to become overcharged and somewhat confused as the craftsmanship loses its assurance (Nos. 71–73).

This change of emphasis is but one symptom of a gradual relaxation of the discipline of the southern style in favour of a less austere influence which appears towards the end of the dynasty, and particularly in the reign of Amen-em-het III (1841–1793? B.C.). The disdainful and arrogant features of the earlier statues become softened into an expression of weariness and disillusion (Nos. 50, 58, 69), though a harsher interpretation is still evident in certain routine products of the Theban workshops. That Egyptian art, at this moment of unification under an unchallenged, centralised monarchy, achieved a parallel synthesis of its main styles will be apparent in the statue of Amen-em-het III from Hawara, which has infused the idealistic mortuary tradition with a searching analysis of character in a realistic style (Nos. 61, 62, 64). This statue is sometimes regarded as representing the king as a young man, but since it comes from his funerary monument and was therefore probably made towards the end of his life, its fresh, unlined features seem to the writer to owe more to the idealism of funerary sculpture. In the portraits of this reign there is little attempt to show the king as being omnipotent, or aloof from human forces; mortal cares seem to bow him down with an almost painful weight: even colossal sculpture shows the same analytical characterisation (No. 63). With them, in fact, we may fairly claim that the Egyptian sculptor transcends the concept of statuary as a repository of superhuman force, and achieves instead an embodiment of human personality. It is not perhaps irrelevant that in contemporary religious thought, with the more widespread development of the Osiris doctrines, the deceased should be regarded less as a materialisation than as a spirit. There comes into Egyptian art at this period a rare harmony of form and content which is as manifest in the cloaked statuary of private persons (Nos. 65–68) as in the sphinxes and other sculptures of the king (Nos. 76–78).

This impressive unity, however, is only achieved for a short while at the climax of the XIIth Dynasty, and then it fades abruptly. It is at the moment difficult to trace any further line of development during the remainder of the Middle Kingdom—the picture is incomplete and very confused. It seems clear, however, that a general cultural decline set in which affected very intimately the arts of the period. The decay was arrested from time to time by more energetic kings who tried to restore a waning prosperity, but such recoveries are only brief. While the Theban school seems to have carried on with the weight of its own momentum for a time, and produced some works of merit in a very formalised style (No. 81), the vigour departed from it eventually, and it lapsed into mannerism (No. 80). Similarly, the Memphite school falls back on its old traditions and declines into vacuity (No. 83). When the Hyksos peoples irrupted into Egypt in the 17th century B.C., it was only the flickering lamp of Middle Kingdom culture that they extinguished.

The art of the Middle Kingdom, the little that has survived from the profusion which has been destroyed, is too often dismissed by its critics as formalistic and static—a dour reaction from the lively naturalism of the Old Kingdom. This view, however, is surely too superficial. Middle Kingdom art was inspired and shaped by the forces of a contemporary culture, which found itself obliged to discard the optimistic belief of a former age that the life on earth was the good life that could be prolonged into eternity. The subjective values which the Middle Kingdom adopted were also expressed in the art of the period, so successfully that it had a particular appeal for a later age which was also seeking a similar mystical passivity. Such art may have lacked the invention and freshness of the Old Kingdom style, and its power may be of a more static kind: but the complete unity which it achieves in its masterpieces, and the impressive force of its portrait statuary, place it high among the most compelling works of man in the Ancient World.

AN OUTLINE OF EGYPTIAN HISTORY TO 1590 B.C.

PREDYNASTIC AGE UP TO 3188 B.C.

In prehistoric times the Nile valley was gradually cultivated by small groups of people who were in transition from a food-gathering to a food-producing economy. Isolated communities, living under the protection of local gods, coalesced into larger units until two separate kingdoms were formed, the North or Lower Egypt, and the South or Upper Egypt, each ruled by a divine king. When the unification of these " two lands " was achieved in historic times, the Egyptians had developed into a well-disciplined people with a system of writing and mensuration and a highly developed social organisation.

ARCHAIC PERIOD, DYNASTIES I-II, 3188-2815 B.C.

Despite a probable struggle for power during this period, the arts of peace were steadily developed.

OLD KINGDOM, DYNASTIES III-VI, 2815-2294 B.C.

With the firm establishment of a centralised government under an absolute monarchy and the adoption of the sun-cult as a State religion, civilisation made a sudden advance and the arts rapidly developed to a pitch of great refinement. Immense pyramid-complexes, mastaba-tombs, and temples were built of stone near the capital at Memphis, and were embellished with statuary and coloured reliefs for the service of dead kings, their families and retainers. These privileges were extended throughout the period to other members of the ruling classes.

FIRST INTERMEDIATE PERIOD, DYNASTIES VII-X, 2294-2134 B.C.

During the latter part of the Old Kingdom, a feudal nobility developed which was strong enough to challenge the central power at the end of the VIth Dynasty. Incursions of Asiatics into the Delta and social revolution hastened the process of decay and impoverishment : and the cultural life of the country was reduced by anarchy and civil war. But about 2240 B.C. a dynasty of princes at Herakleopolis imposed a strong rule over most of the country and directed their efforts to freeing the Delta from foreign domination. An ambitious Theban family took advantage of this to claim some independence.

Dynasty XI, 2134-1991 B.C. A struggle developed between the rival powers of Herakleopolis and Thebes which was waged with varying fortunes by the first four Theban princes of this dynasty, victory finally being achieved by Menthu-hetep II (Neb-hepet-ra) *c.* 2052 B.C., during whose long reign of fifty years Egypt became once more a unified kingdom. The twelve years of his successor, Menthu-hetep III (Se-ankh-ka-ra), saw a steady increase in prosperity; but on his death in 1998 B.C., disorder broke out again and the position remains obscure until the vizier Amen-em-het ascends the throne as the first king of the next dynasty.

Dynasty XII, 1991–1778 B.C. *Chief Kings* : Amen-em-het (Ammenemes) I, Senusret (Sesostris) I, Amen-em-het II, Senusret II, Senusret III, Amen-em-het III.

The peace and order that this dynasty established brought about an improvement in wealth and cultural standards. The administrative fulcrum was shifted to Lisht, and the Faiyum was developed by irrigation and reclamation works into the fertile region it has remained ever since. An aggressive spirit fostered by years of internecine strife was now turned outwards to the conquest of Nubia, which was organised as a trading area : some control was also exercised in Syria. Little is known of the history of the middle years of the dynasty, but it is presumed that the power of the local governors grew to such an extent that it had to be curbed again in the reign of Senusret III.

SECOND INTERMEDIATE PERIOD, DYNASTIES XIII—XVI, 1778-1590 B.C.

In this obscure period, adventurers of all sorts seized power : many of their names exist, but hardly any details of their reigns. Stronger Pharaohs secured some unity for a time; but inevitably the rival dynasty (the XIV?) appeared in the Delta. About 1680 B.C., the country in this weak and divided state fell an easy prey to the Hyksos, a horde of Semitic peoples with probable Aryan elements, who quickly subjugated most of the country, thanks to such superior weapons as their horse-drawn chariot and composite bow. By the end of the period, however, a family of princelings at Thebes had secured some measure of independence for the south.

SUGGESTIONS FOR FURTHER READING

1. BACKGROUND STUDY.

A. Erman: *The Literature of the Ancient Egyptians,* (trans. by A. M. Blackman). London, 1927.

H. Frankfort and Others: *Before Philosophy.* London, 1949.

H. E. Winlock: *Rise and Fall of the Middle Kingdom in Thebes.* New York, 1947.

2. SCULPTURE.

L. Borchardt: *Statuen und Statuetten von Köningen und Privatleuten im Museum von Kairo.* Teil II, Berlin, 1925.

H. G. Evers: *Staat aus dem Stein.* Munich, 1929.

G. Legrain: *Statues et Statuettes de Rois et de Particuliers.* Tome 1, Cairo, 1906.

3. SCULPTURE IN RELIEF.

A. M. Blackman: *The Rock Tombs of Meir.* London, 1914—

E. Naville and H. R. Hall: *The XIth Dynasty Temple at Deir el-Bahari.* London, 1907-13.

P. E. Newberry and F. Ll. Griffith: *El Bersheh.* London, 1894-95.

W. M. F. Petrie: *Koptos.* London, 1896.

4. PAINTING.

N. de G. Davies: *The Tomb of Antefoker.* London, 1920.

N. de G. Davies: *Five Theban Tombs* (The Tomb of Daga). London, 1913.

P. E. Newberry and Others: *Beni Hasan.* London, 1893-1900.

5. JEWELLERY.

G. Brunton: *Lahun I, the Treasure.* London, 1920.

H. E. Winlock: *The Treasure of El Lahun.* New York, 1934.

J. de Morgan: *Fouilles à Dahchour.* Vienna, 1895-96.

6. ARTICLES.

H. Chevrier: *A Twelfth Dynasty Egyptian Shrine,* in *Illustrated London News,* 4th June, 1938, p. 998.

N. de G. Davies: *The Work of the Graphic Branch,* in *Bulletin of Metropolitan Museum of Art, Egyptian Expedition,* 1931-32, pp. 23-29.

W. C. Hayes: *Royal Portraits of the Twelfth Dynasty,* in *Bulletin of Metropolitan Museum of Art,* Dec., 1946.

P. E. Newberry: *Egypt as a Field for Anthropological Research,* in *Report of Ninety-first Meeting, British Association,* 1923, p. 175.

H. E. Winlock: *Excavations at Thebes, Bulletin of Metropolitan Museum of Art, Egyptian Expedition,* 1919-20, pp. 12-32.

DESCRIPTIVE NOTES TO THE PLATES

The measurements given refer only to that part of the object which is illustrated.

The following abbreviations are used to denote the various archæological missions under whose auspices excavations have been conducted : —

B.S.A.E., *British School of Archæology in Egypt and Egyptian Research Account,* London.

E.E.F., *Egypt Exploration Fund,* later (1919) *Egypt Exploration Society,* London.

H-B., *Harvard University-Boston Museum of Fine Arts Egyptian Expedition,* Boston.

I.F.A.O., *Institut Français d'Archéologie Orientale,* Cairo.

M.M.A., *Egyptian Expedition of the Metropolitan Museum of Art,* New York.

S.A., *Service des Antiquités de l'Egypte,* Cairo.

1. STELA OF AN UNKNOWN MAN. White limestone carved in raised relief, hieroglyphs incised. 25 x 18 ins. Excavated by E.E.F. at Dendereh, 1898. Late First Intermediate Period or early XIth Dynasty. At Edinburgh.

   An unknown courtier and his wife Bebi, her arm around him, sit on the left and receive funerary offerings from their sons and daughters. The work is inept and the disposition of the figures and offerings badly managed. Yet this relief has a certain lively vigour, and includes features, such as the jar of ointment held to the nostrils and the mirror in its case under the chair, that belong more to Middle Kingdom iconography. The new artistic vision has, in fact, been formed : only the expression is archaic.
   Photo. Courtesy, Royal Scottish Museum.

2. STELA OF THE CHANCELLOR THETHI. Hard limestone carved in raised relief, hieroglyphs incised. 43 x 33 ins. Acquired from Kurneh area of Thebes, 1902. Early XIth Dynasty. At London.

   Thethi is shown with two subordinate officials receiving the funerary offerings carved on the right in raised relief. This stela, of which only the lower half is here illustrated, shows a very great advance upon the previous specimen, the technique and design being far more accomplished. It reveals in a more refined state the same peculiar features which are characteristic of the Early Middle Kingdom reliefs—the elongated figures, the fragile physiognomy with the long eye and sharply defined thick lips, clean, rather brittle outlines, and a meticulous attention to details as contrasted with broad masses of pattern. The shallow relief shows little attempt at modelling.
   Photo. Courtesy, Trustees of the British Museum.

3. STATUE OF THE CHANCELLOR MESEHTI. Alabaster, traces of paint, eyes inlaid. Height 8¾ ins. Acquired from a tomb at Asyut, 1894. Late First Intermediate Period. At Cairo.

This remarkable little figure came from the cabin of one of Mesehti's model funerary craft: similar statuettes have been found in other tombs at Asyut. It illustrates in a most direct fashion the vigorous, even brutal, force that underlies the contemporary southern art-style, and which was to infuse the art of the Middle Kingdom with an unusual power. The legs splayed apart, the integration of the lower and upper halves by the linking form of the left arm with its massive hand upon the knee, the thick limbs and neck, barely freed from the matrix, give this little statue an abstract force and an intensity that is more "primitive" than the intellectual cubism of most Egyptian sculpture. The hollows and depressions of this statuette are as eloquent as the various formal masses. A unity of form and feeling which is a feature of the best work of the Middle Kingdom is already expressed in this little statue.

Photo. From H. G. Evers: "Staat aus dem Stein," taf. 2, by courtesy of Müncher Verlag, GMBH (bisher F. Bruckmann Verlag).

4. STATUES OF THE STEWARD MERI. Limestone, traces of pigment. Average height 23 ins. Acquired from Kurneh area of Thebes, 1902. Early XIth Dynasty. At London.

These twin statuettes reveal an attempt on the part of the Theban sculptor to observe some of the conventions of the Old Kingdom in the pose of the hands of the left-hand figure, and in the representation of the deceased as wearing different costumes. But the position of the arms folded submissively on the breast of the right-hand figure is novel and more in keeping with the essentially formalised conception of these statues. The same pose is repeated on a fragmentary statue of this date, and finds its most developed expression in the now headless statue that Senusret I had made in honour of his ancestor, Prince Intef.

Photo. Courtesy, Trustees of the British Museum.

5. STATUE OF THE CHANCELLOR NAKHTI. Wood, flesh painted red, garment white, eyes inlaid. Height 61 ins. Excavated by I.F.A.O. at Asyut, 1903. Late First Intermediate Period. At the Louvre, Paris.

This statue, one of a number of which the rest are in Cairo, continues the tradition of the Old Kingdom of representing the deceased in various habits (cp. No. 4). Here he is shown striding forward holding back the flap of his kilt: his left hand once held a baton. The statue is superior to the others found in the same tomb, and well above the average for this period in its skilful if stylised carving and in its large size.

Photo. Courtesy, Archives Photographiques, Paris.

6. STATUE OF QUEEN ASHAYET. Wood, skirt painted red, braces white, bracelets gilded, eyes inlaid. Height 16 ins. Excavated by M.M.A. at Deir el-Bahri, 1920-21. Early XIth Dynasty. At Cairo.

This statuette of a secondary wife of Menthu-hetep II was found in the same coffin as the body of its owner and appears to have been the only specimen of its type in the deposit (cp. No. 5). It doubtless displays the standard of the best workmanship of the early part of that king's reign. The stiff, provincial handling, and the pose with hands held rigidly extended at the sides and with feet placed together, recall the nude figures of women that appear with servant figures in the later tombs of the First Intermediate Period, and are thought by some to represent concubines.

Photo. Courtesy, Metropolitan Museum of Art, New York.

7. STATUES OF OFFERING-BEARERS. Wood, painted. Average height 44 ins. Excavated by M.M.A. at Deir el-Bahri, 1920. Later XIth Dynasty. At Cairo and New York (right-hand figure).

These well-preserved servant statues from the tomb of Meketra are three-dimensional versions of figures that appear in Old Kingdom reliefs showing women bringing produce from the owner's estates (cp. No. 38). The assured but restrained handling of these two figures shows the immense progress that the Theban wood-carver has made in his craft during the reigns of Menthu-hetep II and III.

Photo. Courtesy, Metropolitan Museum of Art, New York.

8. RELIEF OF QUEEN KAWIT. Limestone, carved in sunk relief. 20 x 15 ins. Excavated by E.E.F. at Deir el-Bahri, 1904-5. Early XIth Dynasty. At Cairo.

This scene, showing Queen Kawit drinking a cup of beer while a maid dresses her hair, is part of the external relief decoration of her sarcophagus. The treatment is characteristic of the early part of the reign of Menthu-hetep II, and has its own peculiar appeal. The somewhat stiff, elongated figures are defined by careful drawing and a most exacting technique.

Cairo Museum.

9. RELIEF OF QUEEN ASHAYET. Limestone, carved in sunk relief. 34 x 22 ins. Excavated by M.M.A. at Deir el-Bahri, 1920-21. Early XIth Dynasty. At Cairo.

This scene shows Queen Ashayet seated left, drinking a cup of beer which an attendant pours out for her: on the right, a maidservant holding a goose-wing fan presents her with a vase of myrrh while a pet bitch squats under her chair. This relief, which forms part of the external decoration of her sarcophagus, was almost certainly fashioned by the same craftsman who made Kawit's (cp. No. 8). It is from such precise though formal work that the characteristic southern relief style developed during the Middle Kingdom (cp. Nos. 16, 21).

Photo. Courtesy, Metropolitan Museum of Art, New York.

10–13. FOUR STATUES, from various sites, arranged here for purposes of comparison, showing a king of the early XIth Dynasty and another of the early XIIth Dynasty in the form of a resurrected immortal.

10. STATUE OF KING MENTHU-HETEP II. Sandstone, flesh painted black, costume white, crown dark red. Height 72 ins. Excavated by S.A. at *Bab el-Hosan,* Deir el-Bahri, 1901. Middle XIth Dynasty. At Cairo.

This statue of the king in jubilee costume was found wrapped in mummy bandages in an otherwise empty tomb. It is similar to a pair, now headless, which were placed in the court of his nearby funerary temple. The enormous legs, which are more summarily finished than the rest of the statue, help to emphasise the cubic massiveness of the form, as does the tightly drawn robe undisturbed by any folds. The throne, also, is reduced to a mere cube unrelieved by any decoration; and the high rectangular pedestal emphasises the detachment and aloofness of this stark conception of majesty. There is the same cohesion of form that distinguishes the statuette of Mesehti (cp. No. 3). The garish colouring contributes to an impressive effect of latent barbaric power.

Photo. From H. G. Evers: " Staat aus dem Stein," taf. 12, by courtesy of Müncher Verlag, GMBH (bisher F. Bruckmann Verlag).

11. STATUE OF KING MENTHU-HETEP II. Sandstone, painted. Height 80 ins. Excavated by M.M.A. at Deir el-Bahri, 1925-26. Middle XIth Dynasty. At New York. (The head really belonged to a companion statue, the body of which had been destroyed).

This composite statue gives a more complete impression of the several " Osiride " statues which stood along the avenue of the king's funerary temple and were placed under every tree in the temple courtyard. They are but standing versions of the seated statues (cp. No. 10) showing the king in his jubilee costume. They reveal the same savage intensity of expression and a similar emphasis upon the abstract quality of the cubic forms which underlie the Theban sculpture of the Middle Kingdom.

Photo. Courtesy, Metropolitan Muesum of Art, New York.

12. STATUE OF KING SENUSRET I. Painted limestone. Height 71 ins. Excavated by I.F.A.O. at Lisht, 1895. Early XIIth Dynasty. At Cairo.

This statue showing the king in the guise of Osiris, the god of the dead in the underworld, is one of six that were unearthed in the ruins of the king's funerary temple : fragments of others found in later excavations are in New York. Such Osiride statues had apparently been incorporated into funerary temples in the Old Kingdom, and there is some reason to associate them with the square-pillared architecture of the IVth Dynasty. The Lisht statues represent in their stylised bandage-swathed forms that tendency towards an intellectual architectonic art, the inspira-

36

tional centre of which is probably to be sought at Abydos, a city which from earliest times had been an influential religious centre. Sculpture representing the king as the mummified Osiris should perhaps be distinguished from very similar statues representing the king in his jubilee costume (cp. No. 11), though the distinction is a fine one since the idea of the resurrected Osiris probably derives from the rebirth in jubilee of the divine king, or *vice versa*. Like the seated figures from the same site (cp. Nos. 26, 28), such statues had a part to play in the personal cult of the dead Pharaoh, and they are therefore in the idealistic tradition of Old Kingdom mortuary sculpture, representing the deceased not as the powerful terrestrial ruler but as the Osirian immortal.
Photo. From H. G. Evers: " Staat aus dem Stein," taf. 31, by courtesy of Müncher Verlag, GMBH (bisher F. Bruckmann Verlag).

13. **STATUE OF KING SENUSRET I.** Painted limestone. Height 185 ins. Excavated by S.A. at Karnak, 1910. Early XIIth Dynasty. At Cairo.

This colossal Osiride statue was excavated in the foundations of a later monument and appears to have come originally from a shrine erected for the king's first jubilee. The king is shown with flesh painted black, standing against a pillar, the sides of which are sculptured in high relief, and holding two *ankh* life-signs, presumably symbolising an Osirian resurrection. The hole in the centre of the forehead was for a metal uraeus-serpent.
Photo. From H. G. Evers: " Staat aus dem Stein," taf. 35A, by courtesy of Müncher Verlag, GMBH (bisher F. Bruckmann Verlag).

14. **PAPYRUS-BEARER.** Hard white limestone, painted. 18½ x 18½ ins. Excavated by E.E.F. at Deir el-Bahri in 1903-4. Middle XIth Dynasty. At Geneva.

This specimen gives a good idea of the quality and originality of the reliefs in the funerary temple of Menthu-hetep II at Deir el-Bahri, since it is less sadly shattered than most existing fragments. The scene may be completed from a copy in a private tomb at Meir of the following dynasty. The end of a rope in the top left-hand corner is sufficient for us to see that this figure would have been preceded by others showing men kneeling on all fours so as to get the loads hoisted well on to their shoulders before rising and staggering off with their burdens. Although papyrus-bearers appear in provincial tomb reliefs during the Old Kingdom, this fragment reveals a novel and keenly observed interpretation of the subject. The shallow relief is still in the Theban tradition of the earlier part of the Dynasty (cp. No. 2).
Photo. Courtesy, Musée d'Art et d'Histoire, Geneva.

15. **HEAD OF KING MENTHU-HETEP II.** Hard white limestone carved in raised relief and painted. 14 x 13 ins. Excavated at Deir el-Bahri, 1906. Middle XIth Dynasty. At Edinburgh.

The king is shown wearing a short wig and " boatman's circlet " with streamers and guiding cobras. The sharp, careful cutting of the stone is characteristic of the sculptures of this king's funerary temple at Deir el-Bahri, in which a vigorous and original conception is given form with great precision of line and detail. Note the small ear, a distinctive feature of the work of this dynasty. The hole in the lobe for an ear-ring(?) is also exceptional at this period.

Photo. Courtesy, Royal Scottish Museum.

16–18. RELIEF OF KING MENTHU-HETEP III. Hard limestone. 51 x 32 ins. Acquired by Dr. Henry Abbot between 1843 and 1852 from a temple at Armant near Thebes. Late XIth Dynasty. At Brooklyn, collection of the New York Historical Society.

This raised relief is probably from a jubilee-festival shrine, and shows the king with the goddess Iunyt, Mistress of Memphis, wearing the vulture head-dress. To the left, wearing the Red Crown of Lower Egypt and holding the flail and *nemes* portfolio, he dances before a god under the protection of the divine hawk of Edfu (cp. No. 22). The superb quality of this carving, the delicate low relief, crisp detail and subtle modelling represent XIth Dynasty art at its full development.

Photo. Courtesy, Brooklyn Museum, New York.

19. STATUE OF KING AMEN-EM-HET I. Red granite. Height 46 ins. Found at Tanis by Auguste Mariette 1860-61, re-excavated by E.E.F., 1883. Early XIIth Dynasty. At Cairo.

Only the upper half of this colossal seated statue is shown. The massive modelling of the torso and limbs is in the Upper Egyptian tradition. The bold stylisation of the head nevertheless seems to represent the physiognomy of this king, who was probably of Nubian extraction. A more damaged statue from Mendes reproduces the same characteristic features, the broad face, the high cheekbones and wide jaw. The somewhat brutal intensity of expression should be compared with that of the earlier statues from Upper Egypt (cp. Nos. 10, 11). In certain statues of his son, Senusret I, these facial characteristics are also reproduced to a lesser extent (cp. No. 20).

Photo. From H. G. Evers: " Staat aus dem Stein," taf. 17, by courtesy of Müncher Verlag, GMBH (bisher F. Bruckmann Verlag).

20. STATUES OF KING SENUSRET I. Painted wood, crowns and kilts covered with gesso. Average height 22 ins. Excavated by M.M.A. at Lisht, 1914. Early XIIth Dynasty. At Cairo and New York (right-hand figure).

These uninscribed statues showing the king carrying a sceptre and wearing the crowns of the North and South, seem to be cult-statues used in the burial ceremonies of the vizier Im-hetep, and afterwards interred as sacrosanct material in a special pit near his mastaba-tomb in close proximity to the pyramid of Senusret I. It has been inferred from this circumstance that these statues represent Senusret I; but it cannot be said that they bear a strong resemblance to other statues of this king from the

38

same site (cp. Nos. 12, 26), though they are not unlike certain stylised sculptures from Thebes (cp. No. 27). They therefore probably represent Senusret I as a young man during the early period of his long co-regency. The stocky proportions and more naturalistic pose and treatment differentiate these sculptures from the rather stiffer and more elongated Theban wooden statuary (cp. No. 29).

Photo. Courtesy, Metropolitan Museum of Art, New York.

21. RELIEF OF KING SENUSRET I. Limestone. 77 x 44 ins. Excavated by S.A. at Karnak, 1903. Early XIIth Dynasty. At Cairo.

This relief is from one side of a finely sculptured pillar from a jubilee-festival temple of Senusret I, the ruins of which were employed by a later king as foundation rubble. The scene shows the king being embraced by the god Ptah within a shrine. The clean cutting, precise drawing and skilled craftsmanship are in the tradition of the late XIth Dynasty, but the work is rather bolder and deeper cut and approaches closer to a plastic style than the subtle incised drawing of the Menthu-hetep reliefs, full use being made of shadows cast by the higher relief to achieve a sculptural effect. Such a style appears to have developed in Thebes during the earlier years of the XIIth Dynasty; and similar work of the same group of sculptors may be seen in the reconstructed processional kiosk of Sesostris I at Karnak.
Cairo Museum.

22. RELIEF OF KING SENUSRET I. Limestone, carved in sunk relief, traces of paint. 55 x 40 ins. Excavated by W. M. Flinders Petrie at Coptos, 1893. Early XIIth Dynasty. At University College, London.

The king runs or dances in jubilee regalia before the fertility-god Min, who is not shown in this illustration. The scene is remarkable as being one of the few representations of fairly violent action in Middle Kingdom relief scenes of this date to have survived. The effect of movement and muscular exertion has been most successfully conveyed by the sculptor within the conventions of his art. The portrait of the king does not differ in any essential from portraits in raised relief of his father, Amen-em-het I, from the same site, though presumably these latter should have been carved earlier, perhaps as much as thirty years before. Such a very close resemblance suggests that this relief may have come from a shrine erected during the co-regency with Amen-em-het I, who died soon after celebrating his jubilee, rather than from another and later shrine of Senusret I.
Photo. From F. W. von Bissing: " Denkmäler Agyptischer Sculptur," taf. 34, by courtesy of Müncher Verlag, GMBH (bisher F. Bruckmann Verlag).

23. TORSO OF KING SENUSRET I. Black basalt. Height 40 ins. Acquired in the Faiyum area, 1926. Early XIIth Dynasty. At New York.

The head of this statue was worked separately and dowelled to the body, perhaps as the result of an accident to the original head at the time of carving. It is now missing. The remarkable modelling of the torso seems to be in the best naturalistic Memphite tradition, as is so much of the work in this kind of stone. There is, however, a certain tension in the pose which distinguishes this statue sharply from Old Kingdom specimens.

Photo. Courtesy, Metropolitan Museum of Art, New York.

24. STATUE OF THE LADY SENNUY. Black granite. Height 67 ins. Excavated at Kerma by H-B., 1913-16. Early XIIth Dynasty. At Boston.

Sennuy wears a long, close-fitting garment and holds a flower in her right hand. This statue, which was found in her husband's burial mound in an Egyptian outpost of empire in the Sudan, shows no evidence of the semi-barbarous local art-style and was almost certainly made by metropolitan craftsmen. Like most work in this stone, it combines a restrained sense of form with excellent workmanship and a high finish. The fine quality of this specimen, in fact, suggests that it may well be the work of a royal sculptor, perhaps the gift of the king to an influential governor of his southern domains.

Photo. Courtesy, Museum of Fine Arts, Boston.

25. STATUE OF KING SENUSRET I. Dark grey granite. Height 30 ins. Acquired by Howard Vyse in the Memphis area, *c.* 1839. Early XIIth Dynasty. At London (British Museum).

Despite the unfortunate injuries which this statue has suffered in common with so many of the period, it still gives a very impressive portrait of one of the most forceful monarchs of the XIIth Dynasty. Though the massive handling and firm, uncompromising expression are not in the idealistic tradition of the Lisht statues (cp. No. 26), they nevertheless present a similar physiognomy. The long face with its two-lobed chin differs markedly from the Karnak portraits (cp. No. 27).

Photo. From H. G. Evers: " Staat aus dem Stein," taf. 44, *by courtesy of Müncher Verlag, GMBH (bisher F. Bruckmann Verlag).*

26. STATUE OF KING SENUSRET I. Limestone. Height 21 ins. Excavated by I.F.A.O. at Lisht, 1894. Early XIIth Dynasty. At Cairo.

Upper part of one of ten similar statues found near the ruins of the king's funerary temple. See also No. 28.

Photo. From H. G. Evers: " Staat aus dem Stein," taf. 29, *by courtesy of Müncher Verlag, GMBH (bisher F. Bruckmann Verlag).*

27. STATUE OF KING SENUSRET I. Red granite. Height 122 ins. Excavated by S.A. at Karnak, 1905. Early XIIth Dynasty. At Cairo.

This colossal statue is presumably one of a pair that came originally from a demolished temple of Amen, built by Senusret

I, who perhaps completed the work that his father had begun. It shows the king wearing the White Crown of the South and holding the *nemes* portfolio(?). The broad face, thick lips and heavy beard are in the characteristic style of these " official " sculptures from Karnak, which are well represented by the head of a sphinx found in the same area.

Photo. Courtesy, Lehnert and Landrock Succ., Cairo.

28. **STATUE OF KING SENUSRET I.** Limestone. Height 77 ins. Excavated by I.F.A.O. at Lisht, 1894. Early XIIth Dynasty. At Cairo.

Ten such statues were found near the site of the king's funerary temple, where they had evidently been buried for safety in a later and troubled age. Originally, as many as twenty-four such statues may have been erected in the one of the temple courts. As they are now displayed, ten almost identical statues in close proximity to each other and lacking their proper architectural setting, they give an impression of smooth monotony. But in isolation and good lighting they impress the spectator with their competent, if somewhat academic solution of the problems of monumental sculpture. Even to carve ten such statues, all similar in pose and treatment, without mechanical aids is no mean achievement; and they clearly owe their design and execution to the same master-sculptor and his team of craftsmen. The portraits may lack the force of the hard stone sculpture, but their function is different—not to impress and overawe the living, but to serve as funerary equipment for the personal benefit of the dead king. So far from betraying any realistic conception of statuary, they appear to belong to the idealistic Memphite tradition of Old Kingdom mortuary sculpture. The seat in the form of a stark cube, relieved by a severely balanced heraldic relief, introduces a contrast to the naturalistic rhythm of the human figure. This architectonic discord is avoided in a later version of the same type of statue (cp. No. 64).

Photo. From H. G. Evers: " Staat aus dem Stein," taf. 27, by courtesy of Müncher Verlag, GMBH (bisher F. Bruckmann Verlag).

29. **STATUE OF IMERET-NEB-ES.** Wood, painted, eyes inlaid, wig detachable. Height 34 ins. From the former Anastasi Collection 1828. Probably from Thebes. Early XIIth Dynasty. At Leiden.

This statue, which appears to be the earliest representation of a high priestess of the Theban god, Amen—an office which in later times was held by the queen herself—is, as one would expect, of superior workmanship. An unusual feature for statues of this type is the forward striding pose; but the formal treatment of the face, and the hands extended stiffly at the sides are in the tradition of tomb statues of women from the preceding

41

dynasty (cp. No. 6) and suggest that the Theban school of wood-carvers had steadily evolved its own characteristic style.

Photo. Courtesy, Rijksmuseum van Oudheden, Leiden.

30. STATUETTE OF A FOREIGN WOMAN AND CHILD. Wood, remains of painted gesso coating. Height 6 ins. Excavated by John Garstang at Beni Hasan, tomb of Useri, 1902-3. XIIth Dynasty. At Edinburgh.

This unique statuette of a woman carrying her child in a shawl across her shoulders seems to be a translation in three-dimensional form of figures found in contemporary paintings at Beni Hasan showing foreigners going down into Egypt. A hole in the top of the head suggests that a pot or bundle was once carried there. Deterioration due to wartime storage made the removal of decayed gesso from the face desirable, and the opportunity was taken of restoring the right hand and the tip of the left foot, and of repainting the features. This little figure is much better carved than the majority of servant statues of this size. It is in a hard local wood, the knot holes of which had been stopped up with plaster. The illustration does not reveal the carving of the left arm which evidently was held behind the back under the gown as though supporting the weight of the child—hence the thrusting forward of the head and neck.

Photo. Courtesy, Royal Scottish Museum.

31. DOLLS. Blue faience, details in manganese purple. Average height 4¾ ins. Excavated by M.M.A. at Lisht, 1934. Early or Middle XIIth Dynasty. At Cairo and New York (second from right).

These figurines showing girls wearing jewellery and dressed in various patterned garments held up by shoulder-straps (the second from the left is tattooed only) were found in the filling of the same tomb that yielded the ivory toy dwarfs (cp. No. 32). They may therefore represent dolls for the use of the girl Hepy who had usurped the tomb: but alternatively they may have been magic concubine-figures belonging to the original male owner of the tomb. They are probably the best examples of a faience artefact which was not uncommon in the Middle Kingdom.

Photo. Courtesy, Metropolitan Museum of Art, New York.

32. DANCING DWARF. Ivory. Height 2½ ins. Excavated by M.M.A. at Lisht, 1924. Early or Middle XIIth Dynasty. At New York.

This figurine was found with three other similar dwarf figures, now at Cairo, which formed part of an ivory toy(?) which could be actuated by strings so as to make the figures revolve and pirouette. All are remarkable for the intensity and liveliness of their different poses and facial expressions. The dwarf here illustrated is shown wearing a bandolier and clapping his hands as he takes part in the sacred dances that were usually performed by such persons. The naturalism displayed in these figures is outside the main stream of Egyptian tradition, though apparently connected with the better-class carvings of servants and underlings. This little figure shows that when the Egyptian was untrammelled by conventional ideas of art and its purpose, his vision was essentially realistic.

Photo. Courtesy, Metropolitan Museum of Art, New York.

33. HEAD OF A WOMAN. Wood, traces of paint, gesso and gilding. Height 3½ ins. Excavated by M.M.A. at Lisht, 1907. Early XIIth Dynasty. At Cairo.

The separately worked wig (cp. No. 29) is painted black and decorated with squares of gold leaf to simulate the gold tubes which women of high rank threaded upon their tresses at this period. A subtle, naturalistic modelling gives an austere refinement to the features: the inlaid eyes are missing.

Photo. Courtesy, Cairo Museum.

34–37. FOUR STATUES, from various sites, arranged here for purposes of comparison, showing variations on the theme of the seated figure, whether used as a funerary statue or as an *ex voto*.

34. STATUETTE OF THE STEWARD OF LOWER EGYPT KHETI. Dark granite. Height 8 ins. Excavated by Auguste Mariette at Abydos, 1859. Middle XIIth Dynasty. At Cairo.

This statue shows a variation on the more usual squatting pose where the owner sits tailor-fashion (cp. No. 35). Kheti is clothed in a long cloak, which he holds around him and which reduces the form of his body to a conoid mass. The portraiture of the face is in the same formalised style as befits its small size, and the whole statuette has a monumental unity out of proportion to its modest dimensions.

Photo. From H. G. Evers: " Staat aus dem Stein," taf. 97B, by courtesy of Müncher Verlag, GMBH (bisher F. Bruckmann Verlag).

35. STATUE OF AMENY. Black basalt. Height 15 ins. Acquired in 1853. Provenance unknown. Late XIIth Dynasty. At London.

This is a very good example of the most popular type of votive statue which developed throughout the period, and shows the owner squatting tailor-fashion in a long kilt which is stretched tight across his legs.

Photo. Courtesy, Trustees of the British Museum.

36. STATUE OF THE TREASURER HETEP. Dark granite. Height 29 ins. Excavated at Sakkara by S.A., 1920. Middle XIIth Dynasty. At Cairo.

This curious statue was found in its chapel in the mastaba which Hetep built with materials taken from a nearby VIth Dynasty tomb. It is not unique: a companion statue of limestone occupied a second chapel; and in an adjoining mastaba of about the same date, two similar statues were also found. It has been claimed that these statues may be archetypes of the squatting block statue that developed during the Middle Kingdom and

43

became so popular in later ages (cp. Nos. 37, 75); but it seems more probable that they are local three-dimensional versions of a scene from Old Kingdom reliefs showing the owner in a carrying-chair before a table of offerings. The companion limestone statue shows clearly that Hetep is squatting within such a chair with his knees drawn up and wearing a kilt which leaves his forelegs bare: his arms, too, are shown exposed; and such nudity should be compared with the carefully cloaked forms of the block statues (cp. No. 75). Hetep revived a number of Old Kingdom architectural features in his tomb and the design of these statues appears equally to owe its inspiration to an antiquarian study of the reliefs of a former age. The style of the offering-formulæ on these statues suggest that they are to be dated to the reign of Amen-em-het II, by which time the block statues were fully developed (cp. No. 37).
Cairo Museum.

37. STATUE OF THE TREASURER SI-HATHOR. Limestone, painted. Height 16 ins. From Abydos. Acquired 1856(?), ex-Anastasi Collection. Middle XIIth Dynasty. At London.

This statue appears to be the earliest surely dated specimen in stone of the squatting form of " block " statue. It normally reposes in a niche in Si-hathor's stela; and from a comparison with other stelae of this type, we may infer that such monuments were probably developed at Abydos primarily as *ex votos* for use in the Osiris temple, whence their popularity rapidly spread to other centres. They seem to have their origin in the squatting figurines that appear, during the First Intermediate Period, on the decks of model funerary craft for making the pilgrimage to Abydos. These statuettes represent sacerdotal guardian figures or mourners, often bearded and wearing a wig and a special kind of short cloak, similar to the king's jubilee robe (cp. No. 11), which is also worn by a certain funerary priest known as " the great servant " or " the great one of the god," and which in the squatting position completely clothes the figures except for the feet and hands. Wooden figurines of this type appear in the company of statuettes of Isis and Nephthys, or actresses impersonating these goddesses, weeping at the head and foot of the coffin of the deceased; and suggest some connection with the ritual of the Osiris cult. The highly stylised, swathed form of the block statue consorts well with certain chthonic elements in the Osiris religion. See also Nos. 36, 75.
Photo. Courtesy, Trustees of the British Museum.

38. OFFERING BEARERS. Wood, painted. Height 17 ins. Length 27 ins. Excavated by H-B. at El-Bersheh, 1915. Later XIIth Dynasty. At Boston.

This servant group is from the same tomb that yielded the remarkable painted coffin (cp. Nos. 48, 49) and, like it, is of finer workmanship than the majority of the accompanying objects. The procession is headed by a priest bearing a wine-jar

on his shoulder, and holding a mirror in its case. He is followed
by two women carrying baskets on their heads and grasping
ducks in their right hands. The rear is brought up by a third
woman who has lost her burden: judging by the position of her
arms, this was probably a calf carried across the shoulders.
Photo. Courtesy, Museum of Fine Arts, Boston.

39. SPHINX OF AMEN-EM-HET II. Red granite. Height 81 ins.
Length 189 ins. Former Salt Collection, 1826. Probably from
Tanis. Middle XIIth Dynasty. At the Louvre, Paris.

This sphinx is of orthodox pattern (cp Nos. 77, 78), having
the body of a lion and the head of the reigning monarch, who
in this case has been identified on stylistic grounds as Amen-em-
het II. No other portraits of this king have been definitely
identified. The inscriptions were altered or added by later kings
as on nearly all the monuments found at Tanis. The summary,
restrained carving of this sphinx is exactly suited to the rather
coarse nature of the granular stone and the great size of the
specimen: yet for all its broad treatment, the portrait gives
a masterly impression at once of regal dignity and personal
character. With the sculpture of this middle period of the XIIth
Dynasty, we encounter a classical style which seems to draw its
inspiration from the work of the IVth Dynasty kings, who were
the first to introduce sculptures of sphinxes on a colossal scale
and to work out the typical dynastic form of the lion and sphinx.
Photo. Courtesy, Archives Photographiques, Paris.

40. HEAD OF KING AMEN-EM-HET II. Detail of the sphinx
illustrated in No. 39.
*Photo. From H. G. Evers: "Staat aus dem Stein," taf. 50, by
courtesy of Müncher Verlag, GMBH (bisher F. Bruckmann
Verlag).*

41. STATUE OF KING SENUSRET II. Black granite. Height
82 ins. Excavated by Auguste Mariette, 1860-61(?). Middle
XIIth Dynasty. At Cairo.

Like No. 46, this statue has been usurped by Ramesses II.
It shows evidence, too, of having been inspired by certain Old
Kingdom traditions. Its back-pillar is surmounted by crowned
hawks, recalling the Khephren and Pepy I statues, and the
personal though idealised portraiture is in the classical style of
the IVth Dynasty. Its beautifully polished surface, however, is
in contrast to the painted finish given to most Old Kingdom
statuary. See also No. 43.
Photo. Courtesy, Cairo Museum.

42. UPPER PART OF A STATUE OF KING SENUSRET II.
Grey granite. Height 12½ ins. Acquired in the Memphis area,
1892. Middle XIIth Dynasty. At Copenhagen.

This uninscribed statue has been accredited on stylistic grounds
to Senusret II, and certainly the broad face and rather small
mouth seem to be characteristic of other statues ascribed to this

king. Its restrained, forceful style, like that of most existing contemporary royal portraits, appears to belong to an Upper Egyptian school of hard stone sculpture.

Photo. Courtesy, Ny Carlsberg Glyptotek, Copenhagen.

43. UPPER PART OF A STATUE OF KING SENUSRET II. Detail of the statue illustrated in No. 41.

Photo. Courtesy, Cairo Museum.

44. UPPER PART OF A STATUE OF QUEEN NEFERT. Black granite. Height 44 ins. Upper part found by Auguste Mariette at Tanis, 1860-61; lower part recovered in 1904. Middle XIIth Dynasty. At Cairo.

This statue of the wife of Senusret II has lost the inlaid eyes and has suffered the destruction of the lower part and other damage. The asymmetry caused by the position of the left arm is unusual and suggests that this statue may have been balanced by a companion which, though carved separately, formed the other half of a unified group. The same high polish that characterises the royal sculpture of this reign has been applied to the surfaces of this statue.

Photo. Courtesy, Cairo Museum.

45. UPPER PART OF A STATUE OF QUEEN NEFERT. Black granite. Height 21 ins. Found by Auguste Mariette at Tanis, 1863(?). Middle XIIth Dynasty. At Cairo.

This detail shows the head of a similar, highly polished statue of Queen Nefert which, however, is more complete and shows a more orthodox pose of the hands resting flat above the knees. The queen is shown wearing a pectoral of the type illustrated in No. 71. The technique of both statues is superb, the intractable stone having been carved, incised and polished with complete assurance and mastery. This group of royal statues reveals the full flower of the classical art of the Middle Kingdom in all its aloof austerity.

Photo. From H. G. Evers: " Staat aus dem Stein," taf. 73, by courtesy of Müncher Verlag, GMBH (bisher F. Bruckmann Verlag).

46, 47. STATUE OF KING SENUSRET II. Dark granite. Height 104 ins. Excavated by Auguste Mariette at Tanis, 1860-61(?). Middle XIIth Dynasty. At Cairo.

This colossal statue, which has been usurped in a later age by Ramesses II (1292-1226 B.C.) who cut his barbarous cartouches and pectoral unfeelingly upon the superb work of his predecessor, has been accredited most plausibly to Senusret II on stylistic grounds. The pose, with the clenched hand held upright on the knee, differs from that adopted in the earlier part of the dynasty and recalls the IVth Dynasty style. The back-pilaster (cp. No. 41) distinguishes this statue from those of Senusret I (cp. No. 23). In the work of this period, in fact, there seems more evidence of an antiquarian return to the Pharaonic traditions of

Old Kingdom statuary though the massive modelling of the body and the forceful, stern portraiture belong to the Theban style of the Middle Kingdom.

Photo. Courtesy, Cairo Museum.

48. COFFIN PAINTING. Painted wood. 13 x 8 ins. Excavated by H-B. at El-Bersheh, 1915. Later XIIth Dynasty. At Boston.

This scene is painted upon the bare cedar-wood of the outer coffin of Tehuti-nakht in thick, brilliant colours which have an enamel-like gloss characteristic of this class of work. The scene, which is from the left-hand interior face, shows the owner seated on the left, being censed by an attendant priest and surrounded by funerary offerings. This style of painting, which is also found in other rare instances at Bersheh and Meir, is unusual in revealing a painter-like technique, form being expressed by colour rather than line, and with an evident delight in brush-work. The nearer leg is painted a lighter shade of red; and a line, so thick as to be almost a shadow, defines the shape of the nearer arm.

Photo. Courtesy, Museum of Fine Arts, Boston.

49. COFFIN PAINTING. Painted wood. 9 x 6 ins. Excavated by H-B. at El-Bersheh, 1915. Later XIIth Dynasty. At Boston.

This detail from the same coffin shows a more conventional treatment in the painting of the plumage of the two duck-offerings, though the use of outline is restricted and the form is built up by patterns of bold, but harmonious, colour rather than by line.

Photo. Courtesy, Museum of Fine Arts, Boston.

50. STATUE OF KING SENUSRET III. Dark grey granite. Height 55 ins. Excavated by E.E.F. at Deir el-Bahri, 1905. Late XIIth Dynasty. At London.

This statue is one of six that probably had been erected on the upper platform of the southern Court of the XIth Dynasty temple at Deir el-Bahri. All have been broken off above the knees: four have well-preserved heads which vary greatly in expression. It has been claimed that these differing portraits represent the king at various ages, though it is apparent that they were carved at about the same time. One of the statues is in Cairo, the remaining three statues with heads are in London. Most portraits of Senusret III represent him with considerable vigour as a stern, somewhat disillusioned potentate; and this statue is no exception to the rule. A good deal of the saturnine expression, however, disappears when the head is seen from eye-level (cp. No. 51).

Photo. Courtesy, Trustees of the British Museum.

51. HEAD OF KING SENUSRET III. Detail of the statue illustrated in No. 50.

Photo. From H. G. Evers: " Staat aus dem Stein," taf. 85, by courtesy of Müncher Verlag, GMBH (bisher F. Bruckmann Verlag).

52, 53. HEADS OF CANOPIC JARS. Gypsum, traces of pigment.
Average height 4¾ ins. Excavated by B.S.A.E. at Illahun, 1920.
Middle XIIth Dynasty. At Edinburgh.

These heads came from the mastaba-tomb of an unknown man
near the pyramid of Senusret II. The unusual nature of the
stone suggests that these heads were made locally in the Faiyum.
The eyes are outlined in black, the pupils are brown, and the
caruncles are shaded in red. The hair was represented by a
thick coat of blue pigment which has largely disappeared. The
semi-translucent stone gives a delicate wax-like quality to these
representations of the features of the deceased.

Photo. Courtesy, Royal Scottish Museum.

54. ENGRAVED AMULETIC KNIFE. Ivory. Length 6 ins.
Acquired in 1921 from the Theban(?) area. XIIth Dynasty. At
Edinburgh.

The part here illustrated of an unfinished knife of hippopotamus ivory shows at its best the quality of Egyptian drawing
and engraving at this period—restrained, firm and precise. The
symbols engraved—the eye of the sun-god, protective amulets, a
Seth-headed animal with arrow-tipped tail, a baboon carrying
a lamp—have been incised with no hesitancy and with very little
indication of the beginning and end of each burin-troke. Recent
studies suggest that these implements, formerly called " wands,"
are to be regarded as magical knives for protecting the owner
from the bite of snakes or poisonous insects.

Photo. Courtesy, Royal Scottish Museum.

55. HIPPOPOTAMUS. Blue-glazed faience, details in manganese
purple. Length 6⅝ ins. Provenance unknown. Collection of Mr.
and Mrs. Bradley Martin, 1948, on loan to the Brooklyn
Museum. Early or Middle XIIth Dynasty.

The hippopotamus had been an important and sacred food
animal in Egypt in prehistoric times; but by the Old Kingdom,
it appears to have been hunted solely for sport. Scenes representing the hunting of the beast in the marshy pools of the Nile
occur in reliefs of the period and persist, perhaps as a convention throughout historic times. In the Middle Kingdom, substitutes for such scenes, or supplements of them, appear in the form
of faience sculptures showing the hippo either lurking among the
aquatic plants of his normal surroundings or rearing up at bay
to bellow defiance. Perhaps a humorous regard for Behemoth on
the part of the Egyptian is to be seen in these representations
of the ungainly bulk of the beast, whose grossness is further
emphasised by the delicate plants and even butterflies and birds
that bedeck his flanks, and the open lotus-flower applied almost
like a prize-winning rosette to the expanse of his rump.

Photo. Courtesy, Brooklyn Museum, New York.

56. INNER COFFIN OF THE STEWARD KHNUM-HETEP.
Wood, covered with gesso, gilded and painted, eyes inlaid.
29 x 18 ins. Excavated by B.S.A.E. at Deir Rifa near Asyut,
1907. Late XIIth Dynasty. At Edinburgh.

The upper part of this coffin shows the gilded portrait mask of the deceased wearing a heavy wig, bead "hawk" collar, and the beard of Osiris, in whose idealised form the deceased is represented. Such inner coffins begin to appear towards the end of the Middle Kingdom and finally oust the rectangular coffin from favour.

Photo. Courtesy, Royal Scottish Museum.

57. STATUE OF KING SENUSRET III. Grey granite. Height 48 ins. Excavated by I.F.A.O. at Medamud near Karnak, 1925. Late XIIth Dynasty. At the Louvre, Paris.

This statue, which lacks the lower part and has suffered other damage, represents the king as a young man with none of the lines and sagging muscles of his later age (cp. No. 58), though magnificent statues of this type were also found upon the same site.

Photo. Courtesy, Archives Photographiques, Paris.

58. HEAD OF KING SENUSRET III. Red quartzite. Height 6½ ins. Provenance unknown. Acquired 1926, ex-Carnarvon Collection. Late XIIth Dynasty. At New York.

This fragment may be recognised as portraying the features of Senusret III. The harsh, bitter expression of the granite sculptures has been replaced by a pensive melancholy, which may be partly due to the fact that statuary in this particular stone, which was quarried near Memphis, appears to be the work of a northern school of sculptors who softened and refined the more eruptive vigour of the Theban craftsmen.

Photo. Courtesy, Metropolitan Museum of Art, New York.

59. HEAD OF KING AMEN-EM-HET III(?). Greenish-black basalt. Height 19 ins. Acquired in Egypt, 1894. Provenance unknown. Late XIIth Dynasty(?). At Copenhagen.

The plastic style of Middle Kingdom hard stone sculpture had a special appeal in a later age (cp. No. 81), when it was not only copied very faithfully but occasionally usurped as well. The head here illustrated, like certain other specimens, is dated by some authorities to this later period; and in the absence of some laboratory means of determining the age of carved stone, it does not seem possible to resolve the problem entirely on stylistic grounds alone. The writer is one of those who are of the opinion that this head represents a Middle Kingdom monarch, probably Amen-em-het III, and that it shows an antiquarian return to some of the traditions of the Old Kingdom in such features as the shape of the White Crown and the choice of stone. The handling seems to be in the style of a similar head in diorite at Washington which has been dated very plausibly to the Old Kingdom. The Copenhagen specimen also bears a resemblance to other heads attributed to Amen-em-het III and to the Tanis sphinxes (cp. No. 77) where the same peculiar depressions are carved under the lower lip in order to accentuate the musculature of the chin.

Photo. Courtesy, Ny Carlsberg Glyptotek, Copenhagen.

60. WOMEN WEAVING. Painting on plaster. 40 x 26 ins. From the facsimile by Norman de G. Davies. Middle XIIth Dynasty. Tomb of Khnum-hetep at Beni Hasan.

This faithful copy is of a scene from the west wall of the main chamber of tomb No. 3, which has been preserved from the hand of time and the vandal by a covering film of lime deposits. It shows, centre, a woman preparing flax which is being spun into thread by her companion on the right. On the left, two women squat over a horizontal loom pegged to the ground; but according to the conventions of Egyptian drawing it is shown upright. In the background stands the overseer, whose wealth in years and experience and material well-being is shown in the rolls of fat which cover her. The paintings at Beni Hasan were executed by provincial craftsmen who do not display the careful draughtsmanship, the sense of proportion and skilled assurance of Court artists; but they make up for these deficiencies by a more original vision, a vigorous expressiveness and novel colouring—as far at least as the most important tombs are concerned : in the others, the work of the master-hand is merely copied with more or less success.

Photo. Courtesy, Metropolitan Museum of Art, New York.

61, 62. HEAD OF KING AMEN-EM-HET III. Details of the statue illustrated in No. 64.

Photo. From H. G. Evers: "Staat aus dem Stein," taf. 103, 104, by courtesy of Müncher Verlag, GMBH (bisher F. Bruckmann Verlag).

63. HEAD OF KING AMEN-EM-HET III. Grey granite. Height 30 ins. Excavated by E.E.F. at Bubastis, 1888. Late XIIth Dynasty. At London.

The lower part of the colossus from which this head came is also in the British Museum. It has been usurped by a later king, but the head is now generally accepted as representing the features of Amen-em-het III. Despite the huge size of the specimen, the masterly handling of the stone is extremely faithful and pays due regard to the proportions of the facial structure and its underlying muscles, without degenerating into a timid or over-elaborate statement.

Photo. Courtesy, Trustees of the British Museum.

64. STATUE OF KING AMEN-EM-HET III. Yellow limestone. Height 63 ins. Found in 1895 while digging a canal near the ruins of the king's funerary temple at Hawara. Late XIIth Dynasty. At Cairo.

This statue, though found broken in several pieces and still lacking the tips of the toes, is unusually complete for this period. Like the funerary statues of Senusret I (cp. Nos. 26, 28), it appears to have been conceived and executed in the Memphite tradition of mortuary sculpture and reveals all the idealising tendencies of such statuary. It differs, however, from the Senusret sculptures in achieving a greater unity between the archi-

tectural form of the throne and the organic form of the seated figure by such devices as the back pillar and the inscriptions on the front of the seat by the legs.
Cairo Museum.

65–68. Four differently posed statues of private persons from the latter part of the XIIth Dynasty. All show the main features of the art of the period—careful workmanship, a restrained feeling for form in repose and a unity between an idealised portrait head and a stylised body.

65. STATUE OF THE ROYAL HERALD MENTHU-AO. Black granite. Height 43 ins. Acquired by purchase in first half of 19th century: from Memphis(?). Late XIIth Dynasty. At London.

This statue is more usually dated to the XIth Dynasty, but the material, style and workmanship are clearly of a more sophisticated age. A man with the same name and titles and a similarly named mother erected a stela at Abydos in the 13th year of Senusret III, and there seems no reason to doubt that this statue is of the same important official. Although Menthu-ao is shown uncloaked, there is the same unity of treatment in the broad masses of the face and body that distinguishes the sculptures of the clothed figures of this period.
Photo. Courtesy, Trustees of the British Museum.

66. STATUETTE OF AN UNKNOWN MAN. Limestone. Height 9¼ ins. Provenance unknown. Later XIIth Dynasty. At Brooklyn.

This statue is on a smaller scale than the others in this group but shows the same monumental character.
Photo. Courtesy, Brooklyn Museum, New York.

67. STATUE OF THE STEWARD HETEP. Brown crystalline sandstone. Height 30 ins. From the neighbourhood of Asyut. Late XIIth Dynasty. In the collections of the former Egyptian Museum, Berlin.
Photo. Courtesy, Dr. Rudolf Anthes, Berlin.

68. STATUE OF THE CHIEF PROPHET AMEN-EM-HET-ANKH. Brown crystalline sandstone. Height 29 ins. Provenance unknown. Late XIIth Dynasty. At the Louvre, Paris.

Despite the unusual stance for this period, little real movement is expressed; the figure balances, it does not stride. The heavy wig, long kilt and the position of the hands help to preserve a monumental formalism. The feet are restored.
Photo. Courtesy, Archives Photographiques, Paris.

69. HEAD OF KING AMEN-EM-HET III. Serpentine. Height 4⅞ ins. Acquired 1941, ex-Raphael Collection. Provenance unknown. Late XIIth Dynasty. At Cambridge.

This little head shows the interest of the Middle Kingdom sculptor in material for its own sake, the mottled dark-green stone being given a high polish. It has been attributed to Amen-em-het III and seems to represent him as a young man, the

51

resemblance in profile to the Hawara portrait being particularly close (cp. Nos. 61, 62).

Photo. Courtesy, the Syndics of the Fitzwilliam Museum, Cambridge.

70. HEAD OF KING AMEN-EM-HET III. Black granite. Height 5¼ ins. Acquired 1949, perhaps originally from Medamud, near Karnak. In the Collection of Mr. Albert Gallatin, New York. Late XIIth Dynasty.

This head bears a marked resemblance in profile to a small head in green stone in the former Berlin Collections, which is usually accepted as being of Amen-em-het III. Its features are also similar to those of the obsidian head in the possession of M. Gulbenkian, which is generally regarded as representing the same king. The simple " two-stripe " wig-cover is more common in the following dynasty, but already appears in certain granite statues of Amen-em-het III found at Karnak.

Photo. Courtesy, Brooklyn Museum, New York.

71–73. Specimens of royal jewellery from the tombs of princesses at Dahshur and Illahun. All show the same basic technique—a gold plate is pierced and formed with cloisons for holding the coloured stone inlays, the plain back being most exquisitely chased and worked. Egyptian jewellery, which technically and artistically must be classed among the best ever produced, makes its effect by the contrast of rich, semi-translucent colours and burnished goldwork: the sparkle, or rarity of the gems used is of subordinate consideration to the glowing colour of the entire jewel. The Egyptian jeweller was not content to reproduce one or two stereotyped designs, but devised fresh patterns with each change of king in order to take into account different royal names and titularies.

71. PECTORAL OF KING SENUSRET II. Gold, inlaid with lapis lazuli, carnelian, turquoise and garnet. Height 1¾ ins. Excavated by B.S.A.E. at Illahun, 1914. Middle XIIth Dynasty. At New York.

This breast ornament is in the form of the king's name in an oval cartouche supported by hawks wearing the sun's disk upon their heads and upheld by a kneeling god holding notched palm branches, and other symbols. This combination of devices forms a kind of motto which may be interpreted as, " The Sun-god has granted an eternity of life to King Senusret II." The strength and purity of design, which was meant to be seen at a respectful distance, are matched by the exquisite goldwork and the minute and accurate inlay which is best appreciated at close quarters. This superb specimen is probably the most technically brilliant of all the fine jewellery which has survived from this period. A pectoral of similar design with the name of Amen-em-het III was found with the same deposit, but shows far less skilful workmanship.

Photo. Courtesy, Metropolitan Museum of Art, New York.

72. **PECTORAL OF KING SENUSRET III.** Gold inlaid with lapis lazuli, camelian and turquoise. Height $2\frac{1}{2}$ ins. Excavated by S.A. at Dahshur (south of Sakkara), 1894. Late XIIth Dynasty. At Cairo.

This breast ornament, the chased back of which is shown here, is in the form of a kiosk supported by lotus columns, with figures of the king as crowned griffins trampling and striking down foreign foes at the same time as they support the name of the king : over all hovers the vulture goddess Nekhebet. This pectoral lacks the clarity that distinguishes the design of the previous example, but shows great technical mastery, and makes an ingenious use of the various symbols such as the inclining lotus flowers and the protecting vulture to produce a mechanically perfect jewel.

Cairo Museum.

73. **PECTORAL OF KING AMEN-EM-HET III.** Gold inlaid with coloured stones. Height 3 ins. Excavated by S.A. at Dahshur (south of Sakkara), 1894. Late XIIth Dynasty. At Cairo.

The reverse of this pectoral is shown here to reveal the chased gold back and the tubes for threading through the supporting necklace. This specimen, too, is in the form of a shrine, within which are shown figures of the king clubbing enemies while personified hieroglyphs fan him with the breath of life and the vulture goddess hovers protectingly above. The names of the king and the various titularies are worked into a somewhat worried design which is restless rather than clear and falls short of the technical perfection of earlier specimens.

Cairo Museum.

74. **FISH PENDANT.** Gold, over a core of clay(?) retained within. Length $1\frac{9}{16}$ ins. Excavated by B.S.A.E. at Haraga, near Illahun, 1914. Middle XII Dynasty. At Edinburgh.

This pendant, which is shown greatly enlarged in order that the high quality of its detail may be appreciated, represents a Nile fish (species of *barbus*) and was found with four smaller specimens, less well preserved, in the grave of a child. Its superb workmanship is hardly surpassed even by royal jewellery of the period.

Photo. Courtesy, Royal Scottish Museum.

75. **STATUE OF THE CHIEF ACCOUNTANT SENUSRET-SENEB-EF-NI.** Brown quartzite. Height 27 ins. First acquired by Napoleon I on his Egyptian Expedition in 1799. Later XIIth Dynasty. At Brooklyn.

This specimen, which appears to be an *ex voto*, carries the block-statue-cum-stela idea a stage further by having the stela inscription cut upon the front of the statue itself. The dedication, while not to Osiris, is to a death-god of Memphis who at the end of this period becomes identified with Osiris. Like the few examples of this type of statue which can be dated to the XIIth Dynasty, it shows the feet exposed in the front, and the masses of the haunches and arms tensed under the smoothly drawn cloak. A little later, similar statues show the garment draped in such a way as to reduce the body to a mere cube, and the feet and often the hands wrapped—a form which ultimately gains most favour. This particular statue is a most impressive work of art, and reveals a powerful monumental style in the management of the masses of the head and the muscles of the body. A unity which is so characteristic of the best work of the late XIIth Dynasty, informs it. The figure of the wife is not so satisfactory: the sculptor has been obliged to reduce her to doll-like proportions so as not to interfere with the main design: but he has maintained the cohesion of his composition by treating the form in a summary fashion so that it merges to some extent into the mass of the body of the man, and is framed and defined by the doorway formed by the inscription.

Photo. Courtesy, Brooklyn Museum, New York.

76. UPPER PART OF A STATUE OF KING AMEN-EM-HET III. Black granite. Height 39 ins. Excavated by Auguste Mariette at Mit Faris in the Faiyum, 1862. Late XIIth Dynasty. At Cairo.

This unusual statue shows a king, who is almost certainly Amen-em-het III, in a priest's garments—bandolier, leopard-skin robe and heavy necklace—holding two hawk-headed staves. The heavy plaited wig is unique and appears to be of Libyan inspiration. This statue may therefore represent the king in a guise of special significance to the predominantly Libyan character of his Faiyumi subjects.

Photo. From H. G. Evers: " Staat aus dem Stein," taf. 127, by courtesy of Müncher Verlag, GMBH (bisher F. Bruckmann Verlag).

77. SPHINX OF KING AMEN-EM-HET III. Black granite. Height 25 ins. Length 49 ins. Excavated by Auguste Mariette at Tanis, 1860-61(?). Late XIIth Dynasty. At Cairo.

It is now generally accepted that this sphinx, like similar specimens from the same site, represents the Pharaoh Amen-em-het III. It was usurped by Ramesses II and others who have cut their ugly inscriptions on it. The more usual sphinx of Egypt has the body of a lion and the head of the reigning monarch wearing the wig-cover with lappets (cp. No. 39). Where the Tanis sphinxes differ is in being sculptures of lions with the visage of the king in place of the lion mask. This unusual feature has led several Egyptologists to consider them as the work of foreign invaders (who have not otherwise left any monuments) or as made under foreign influence, and to place their date either earlier or later than the XIIth Dynasty. The orthodox sphinx of Egypt represents the king as a form of the sun-god of Heliopolis: and it may be that these Tanis sphinxes provide a variation on this idea in representing the king as one of the other lion-gods of Heliopolis, whence these statues, together with some others, may have been taken in later years by different usurpers. The monumental leonine and regal character of these sculptures places them in a class apart. They have a unity which distinguishes the work of this period so that the usual incongruity of the sphinx-form does not obtrude. The bold modelling of the animal and human musculature and its integration give them a force and impressiveness which have hardly been surpassed. *Cairo Museum.*

78. SPHINX OF KING AMEN-EM-HET III. Detail of the sphinx illustrated in No. 77.
   Photo. From F. W. von Bissing: " Denkmäler Agyptischer Sculptur," taf. 26, by courtesy of Müncher Verlag, GMBH (bisher F. Bruckmann Verlag).

79. STATUE OF KING HOR. Wood, traces of grey paint and gilding. Height, including hieroglyph, 70 ins. Excavated by S.A. at Dahshur, 1894. Late XIIth(?) Dynasty. At Cairo.
   This cult-statue was found in the wooden shrine within which it is shown here, in a pit-tomb near the second pyramid, presumed to belong to Amen-em-het III, at Dahshur; and represents the spiritual aspect of a probable co-regent of that monarch, who died young. It has a religious significance and is in the idealising style of such funerary sculpture. The statue is unusual in that the head, torso and left leg are made in one from the same log, the other limbs being carved separately and attached by tenons. The slender, somewhat elongated forms belong to the elegant distortions of a sophisticated art which is already trembling on the verge of mannerism.
   Cairo Museum.

80. STATUE OF KING SEBEK-HETEP III(?). Red granite. Height 90 ins. Reputed to have come from Shallufa in the Delta, but perhaps originally from Karnak. Acquired by purchase, 1907. XIIIth Dynasty. At London.
   This statue will serve to illustrate the mannerism into which the XIIth Dynasty style degenerated in the subsequent period, when political instability brought about a general economic and cultural decline. The small head with its heavy beard is out of proportion to the body. The flaccid modelling of the shoulders, chest, arms and hands is without any plastic meaning; the wasp-waist exaggerates the heavy hips; and the leg muscles have been reduced to a decorative pattern while the shin-bone has become a sharp brittle ridge. A formula for statue-making has here been followed without any freshness of vision nor any inner conviction. The nose, feet and lower part of the pedestal have been restored.
   Photo. Courtesy, Trustees of the British Museum.

81. STATUE OF THE HERALD OF THEBES, SEBEK-EM-SAU-EF. Black granite. Height 59 ins. From Armant. XIIIth Dynasty. At Vienna, ex-Hapsburg collection from Miramar.
   But for the inscription there would be a great temptation to place this specimen in the Late Period (c. 660-340 B.C.), a fact

which should encourage us to consider revising some similar attributions. The high polish, searching characterisation and strongly formal treatment of statuary of the period of the late XIIth and early XIIIth Dynasties were particularly admired and copied in a subsequent age : but Sebek-em-sau-ef, who was a high official of the court and the brother of a XIIIth Dynasty queen, can be placed in no other period. His long kilt, similar to that worn by viziers, is not seen in all its bellying volume except in a side view. The National Museum of Ireland possesses a fragment of the legs, a cast of which is used to complete the statue in Vienna. Wilkinson, visiting Armant in the earlier half of the last century, described this statue and copied the inscription in his notebooks, a circumstance which enables us to give its provenance, hitherto unrecorded.

Photo. Courtesy, Kunsthistorisches Museum, Vienna.

82. STATUE OF KING SEBEK-HETEP VIII(?). Dark granite. Height 50 ins. Excavated by S.A. at Karnak, 1904. XIIIth Dynasty. At Cairo.

The king is shown seated in jubilee costume holding the crook and flail sceptres. Despite the cubic nature of its underlying forms, this statue lacks the rude force of the early Theban examples (cp. No. 10), though the strength of the idea of re-birth which it embodies is sufficient to lend it a certain vitality. Its vigour, however, is not that of an untamed force seeking a new expression, but of an ageing convention which has been mechanically and not too skilfully followed.

Cairo Museum.

83. SHRINE OF KING NEFER-HETEP I. Limestone. Height 39 ins. Excavated by S.A. at Karnak, 1904. XIIIth Dynasty. At Cairo.

Monuments showing twin figures of kings standing within a shrine-like portico make their appearance in the latter part of the Middle Kingdom, though the type may have an earlier origin. This specimen is better preserved than most, and so far as may be judged from its ruined condition, is of more than average quality for the period. The soft elegance of the forms, however, rather emphasises the academic handling, and the strong tendency to a lifeless stylisation in the portraiture.

Photo. From H. G. Evers: "Staat aus dem Stein," taf. 143, by courtesy of Müncher Verlag, GMBH (bisher F. Bruckmann Verlag).

Printed by Portland Press Ltd., Tottenham Mews, W.1.

1. Stela of an Unknown Man

2. Stela of Thethi

3. The Chancellor Mesehti

4. The Steward Meri

5. The Chancellor
Nakhti

6. Queen Ashayet

7. Offering-Bearers of Meket-ra

8. Sarcophagus of Queen Kawit

9. Sarcophagus of Queen Ashayet

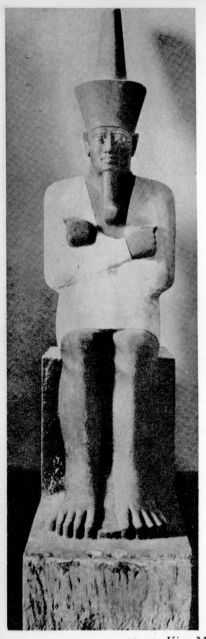

10, 11. King Menthu-hetep II

12, 13. King Senusret I

14. Papyrus-Bearer

15. Head of King Menthu-hetep II

16. Jubilee-Scene of King Menthu-hetep III

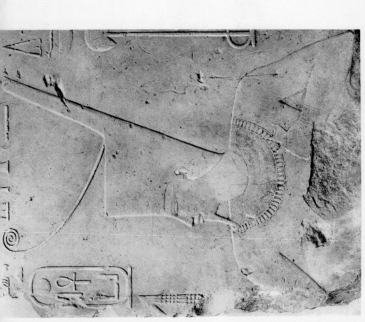

17, 18. Jubilee-Scene of King Menthu-hetep III—details

19. King Amen-em-het I

20. Twin Statues of King Senusret I

21. King Senusret I and the God Ptah

22. King Senusret I Dancing Before a God

23. Headless Statue of King Senusret I

24. The Lady Sennuy

25. King Senusret I

26. King Senusret I—detail

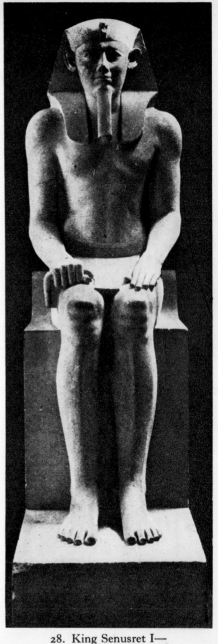

27. King Senusret I—
Karnak

28. King Senusret I—
Lisht

29. Imeret-neb-es   30. Foreign Woman

31. Faience Dolls

33. Head of a Woman

32. Dancing Dwarf

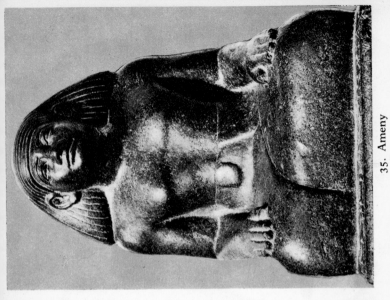

35. Ameny

34. Kheti

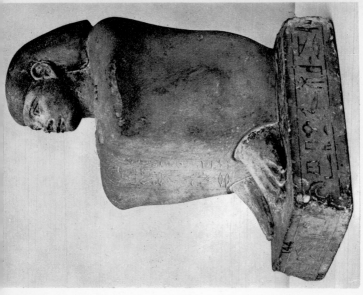

37. Si-hathor

36. Hetep

38. Offering-Bearers

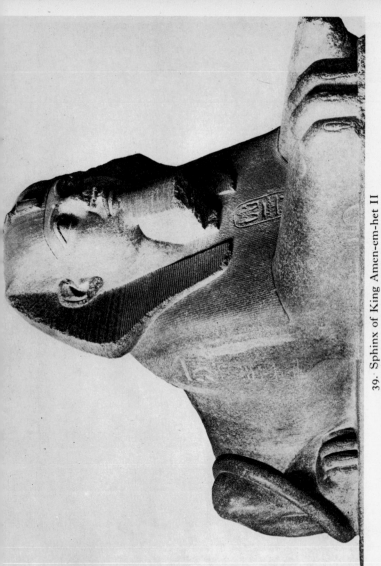

39. Sphinx of King Amen-em-het II

40. Sphinx of King Amen-em-het II—detail

41. King Senusret II

42. King Senusret II

43. King Senusret II—detail

44. Queen Nefert

45. Head of Queen Nefert

46. King Senusret II

47 King Senusret II—detail

48. Scene from Coffin of Tehuti-nakht

49. Duck-Offerings from Coffin of Tehuti-nakht

50. King Senusret III

51. King Senusret III—detail

52. Head of a Canopic Jar

53. Head of a Canopic Jar

54. Ivory Knife—detail

55. Faience Hippopotamus

56. Coffin of Khnum-hetep—detail

57. King Senusret III

58. Head of King Senusret III

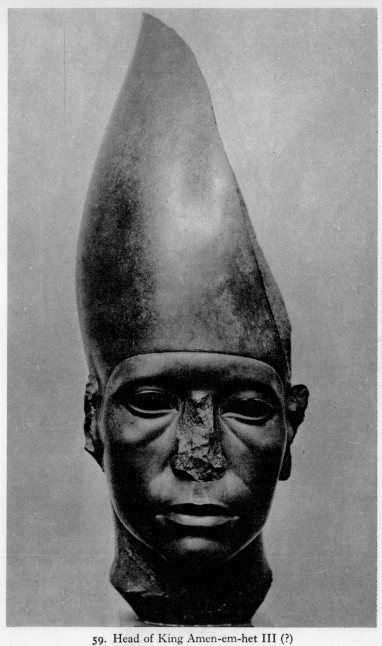

59. Head of King Amen-em-het III (?)

60. Women Spinning and Weaving

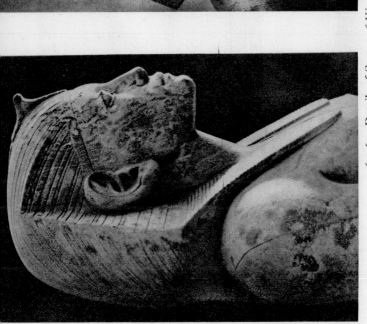

61, 62. Details of Statue of King Amen-em-het III

63. Head of King Amen-em-het III (?)

64. King Amen-em-het III

65. Menthu-ao   66. Unknown Man

67. Hetep   68. Amen-em-het-ankh

69. Head of King Amen-em-het III

70. Head of King Amen-em-het III (?)

71. Pectoral of King Senusret II

72. Pectoral of King Senusret III

73. Pectoral of King Amen-em-het III

74. Gold Fish Pendant

75. Senusret-seneb-ef-ni

76. King Amen-em-het III

77. Sphinx of King Amen-em-het III

78. Sphinx of King Amen-em-het III—detail

79. King Hor   80. King Sebek-hetep III (?)

81. Sebek-em-sau-ef   82. King Sebek-hetep VIII (?)

83. Shrine of King Nefer-hetep I